Colin White & Laurie Boucke

The UnDutchables

**an observation of the Netherlands:
its culture and its inhabitants**

with a little bit of help from:

Michael Nunnally (USA), Huug Schipper/Studio Tint (NL) - line drawings
Darren White (UK) - cover art
Virgil Jorgensen & Associates (USA); BookMasters, Inc. (USA) - production

and the whole Dutch nation, without whose being this would not have been
possible!

Printed In the United States of America

ISBN 0-9625006-1-5

Published by

 colin white &
laurie boucke   P.O. Box 551, Montrose, CA 91021-0551, U.S.A.

PREFACE TO THE SECOND EDITION

The first edition of The UnDutchables has proved more successful than we ever imagined, and in a direction we never thought possible. Originally conceived as a work intended for British tourists, it has yet to sell one copy in that fair Isle.

This second edition corrects and updates some subjects and adds material previously omitted.

As we are now far away from that Magic Kingdom-of-the-Water, and can no longer keep a watchful eye on daily Dutch life, please accept this as THE COMPLEAT UNDUTCHABLES.

February 15, 1991

PREFACE TO THE FIRST EDITION

If you're planning to spend time in Holland, this account will give you an idea of the other side of the ditch.

This work is the result of two persons' experience of living in the Netherlands for a combined total of 22 years of self-imposed exile among the Dutch, affectionately known as CLOGGIES. During our residence, we experienced many facets of Dutch life — THE GOOD, THE BAD AND THE UGLY.

THE GOOD is already reflected in a multitude of works in most western libraries and tourist book shops; THE BAD is reflected in many media reports concerning drug abuse, sexual promiscuity, etc. Some will feel that this work constitutes THE UGLY.

We attempt to focus on the things that the average CLOGGY today holds dear: on the apparent obsession with land, life and liberty . . . the down-to-earth (or rather in this case, down-to-sand) aspects of Living in Holland.

September 20, 1989

Contents

Chapter 1

INTRODUCTION

(THE WAY THE TEXT BOOKS SELL IT)

There

A country (often called Holland) in western Europe bordering on the North Sea, with Belgium on its southern frontier and West Germany on its eastern flank; official language, Dutch; capital, Amsterdam; seat of government, The Hague. Population (1991), 15 million.

Them

The area was occupied by Celts and Frisians who came under Roman rule from the 1st C. BC until the 4th C. AD and was then overrun by German tribes, with the Franks establishing an ascendancy during the 5th-8th C. During the middle ages it was divided between numerous principalities. The northern (Dutch) part (part of the Hapsburg Empire) revolted, in the 16th C, against

Spanish attempts to crush the Protestant faith and won independence in a series of wars lasting into the 17th C., becoming a Protestant republic. The southern part was absorbed into the Spanish Hapsburgs and then in 1713 into the Austrian Hapsburgs. Prior to wars with England and France, the country enjoyed great prosperity and became a centre of art and scholarship as well as a leading maritime power, building up a vast commercial empire in the East Indies, South Africa and Brazil. In the 18th C. it sharply declined as a European power. In 1814 north and south were united, but the south revolted in 1830 and became an independent kingdom (Belgium) in 1839. Luxembourg gained its independence in 1867. The Dutch managed to maintain their neutrality in World War I, but were occupied by the Germans in World War II. The post-war period has seen the country turn away from its traditional dependence on agriculture to emerge as an industrial power and a key figure in the new-look *United Europe*.

NOTE...... The authors acknowledge "**The Oxford Reference Dictionary**", **1986,** for much of the information contained in this Chapter.

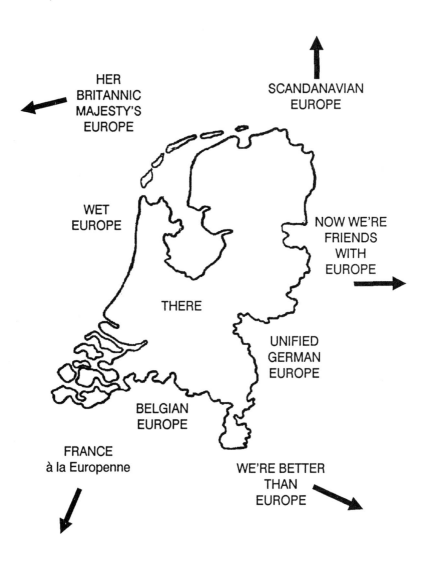

HER
BRITANNIC
MAJESTY'S
EUROPE

SCANDANAVIAN
EUROPE

WET
EUROPE

NOW WE'RE
FRIENDS
WITH
EUROPE

THERE

UNIFIED
GERMAN
EUROPE

BELGIAN
EUROPE

FRANCE
à la Europenne

WE'RE BETTER
THAN
EUROPE

Chapter 2

GETTING ACQUAINTED

Most people only get to visit great works of art . . .
The Dutch get to live in one.

KLM Royal Dutch Airlines
advertisement, 1988.

There

Do not be surprised if one of your first impressions is of being in doll-house country. Everything is small, crowded and cramped: houses, streets, shops, supermarkets, parks, woods, cars, etc. Holland is a densely populated country, and its inhabitants have mastered the art of using the centimetre to its fullest.

This ability and talent has arisen, of course, from the fact that much of the country consists of land reclaimed from the sea. And the reclaiming continues even today.

On an international flight, when the pilot announces that you are flying over Holland — don't blink! You'll miss it, it's that small. You can, in fact, cross the whole nation by car in only three hours.

For those of you arriving by plane from distant lands, a word of advice. Having entered the country and adjusted to the barometric pressure prevalent below sea-level (jet-lag withstanding), you'll undoubtedly want to view the windmills, tulips, cheese markets and canals. Water and horizontal hills abound. So do sex shops. And, yes, you'll see your share of wooden shoes and Frisian cows. These tourist attractions can be exhausted within a day or two.

Them

The inhabitants of this small strip of ex-seabed are not lacking in self-esteem, as reflected in literary titles such as "And the Dutch created the Netherlands" *(En de Neder-landers Schiepen hun Eigen Land)*, "Holland — The New

Atlantis Risen". They are bursting with dikes, nationalism, independence, freedom, equality and political beliefs (Holland boasts at least 29 parties), as will be demonstrated in the ensuing chapters.

The Dutch appear a friendly lot: kind, polite and helpful to tourists. They love to talk about their country and to provide any directions or information you may require. Their fascination with things foreign —products, attitudes, ideas, customs, languages, etc. — is impressive and ego-boosting. The Dutch reputation for tolerance is all too apparent to the foreign visitor. But do not let this image fool you — it changes drastically if you stay long enough to be regarded as *part of the scene.*

The longer you stay, the deeper you sink into it. The dark cloud of disapproval descends as your comrades of the "lowlands" constantly criticize what they consider to be unfavourable situations beyond their borders. There is no relief from this moralizing, despite the fact that similar or even worse situations often exist within their own kingdom.

If you expect to find delicious food or the exotic, forget it. If you like wide, open spaces or a little solitude in nature, this is not the country for you. There are no large forests or wide expanses of land. When walking in the woods, dunes or on the beach, you have the feeling that millions have trod wherever you place your feet. They have. Can this be the stuff that inspired Rembrandt and Van Gogh?

Since most of the country is built on sand, the use of lego-roads is widespread. Streets are paved with bricks which are merely pounded into place. The brick surface has no graded foundation layers. This construction method combined with the Northern European climate guarantees maximum inconvenience for motorists: dips in the roads, sinking tramlines, and a multitude of closed roads while re-flattening/re-surfacing operations are 'in progress.

The Dutch proudly defend the character of their roads. Workmen need only lift up the requisite amount of bricks to reach the work area. One wonders if they would need to lift up any bricks at all if they constructed the roads properly in the first place.

A *cloggy's* prize possession is The Bicycle. It may be a 15-speed ultra-light racing model or a rusty third generation job, honourably handed down through the family. Hence the country is infested with the contraptions.

The Dutch are masters of things connected with water: bridges, dikes, canals, rain, etc. They have had to constantly defend their sand against natural elements with an elaborate survival system, as they will not hesitate to tell you. This defence has been far more successful than that employed against many human foe, as they will neglect to tell you.

Perhaps it's the age-old connection between water and cleansing/purification that drives them to it. Many of them are pathologically obsessed with a form of cleanliness which logically has little connection with practical hygiene. This is especially true of the older generation. It seems the older they grow, the cleaner everything must be.

It should be noted that the older generation appear to be exempt from much of what else follows in this book. Although they are still in full posession of their Dutchness, it does not manifest itself as intensely as before. Perhaps after 60+ years, they are finally prepared to hand the baton to their heirs. Or it may be that most of the elderly have suffered at least one period of extreme hardship, such as having lived under the occupation of a genocide-obsessed **Reich**, which permits them to . . .

**view the world with a
more worldly view.**

Chapter 3

PUBLIC TRANSPORT

In addition to the national train service, Holland, like most countries, utilizes regional bus companies to provide for local public transport. Larger urban areas also have tram systems, and Amsterdam and Rotterdam have a *metro* train service. The public transport system is excellent. It is efficient, modern and comfortable. There are also ample taxis (mainly Mercedes), reasonably priced.

Tickets

The physical size of Holland allows the bus companies to merge their ideas so that the whole country is divided into numbered travel zones. Tickets are valid for a quantity of travel zones and for a specific time, based on the number of zones crossed. You are free to travel anywhere within the defined multi-zone boundary for that period of time.

So far it seems simple. To travel from, say Hilversum to Loosdrecht by bus, one must purchase a ticket for the requisite number of zones. Sorry, but it's not quite as simple as that. Disregarding season tickets, one has two options:

1. Purchase a blank ticket beforehand from a designated shop (post office, tobacconist, train station, etc). The national strip ticket *(strippenkaart)* is divided into a number of lateral strips. A strip ticket can be used on any bus, tram or **metro** in the country. All you need to do is stamp it correctly in one of the yellow boxes provided, or ask the driver to. Knowing how to stamp the ticket correctly is too complex to explain in this account.

2. Purchase a ticket from the driver. This is a less desirable method to use, since this ticket is considerably more expensive, per zone, than one purchased in a shop.

When you join the queue to purchase a train ticket, you will notice a curious sight. After purchasing a ticket, the average *cloggy* takes one side-step (usually to the left) and spends a few moments fiddling before departing with a satisfied look. Foreigners might think the side-step is part of the ticket purchasing process. Wrong. The *cloggies* (male or female) are merely organizing and taking an inventory of their coin purses, and putting their tickets into their handbags. You can also purchase your ticket on board. Depending on circumstances, the price you pay can be:

- the basic ticket price
- the basic price plus a small surcharge
- the basic price plus a hefty fine.

Officially, the ticketless must report to the conductor before the train departs, whereupon the surcharge will be levied. In practice, if you surrender to the conductor voluntarily and he is in a good mood, you'll pay the basic ticket price and perhaps the surcharge. If he discovers the crime, you pay the fine.

Until 1985, tickets were rarely inspected on urban transport. In 1985 it became apparent that the honour system had failed since the transport companies were losing a lot of money.

Groups of inspectors were introduced. At first, the controllers frequently dressed in plain clothes. This uniform was soon eliminated by the democratic Dutch who complained that a *zwart* ("black", fare-evading) passenger should have a fair chance to escape. Now the controllers comprise groups of uniformed youngsters (in their teens or early 20's). A typical team consists of one or two females, one blond Dutchman and a combination of Turks, Surinamese and/or Negroes. These youngsters are often lenient with people who have not stamped their tickets properly.

However, do not be surprised to witness the youngsters frantically tackling a would-be escapee attempting to get out of a *metro* train when it stops at a station. The controllers may grab the person in question. If he tries to escape from their grasp, the train will be delayed for the duration of the struggle on the platform.

Eventually the controllers will drag the escapee back into the train. The doors close and the train proceeds as the escapee passionately protests, "I haven't done anything wrong . . ."

What to Take

All nationalities have their habits and traits when it comes to public transport, especially on longer journeys. The Russians may take vodka or a chess set. Some nationalities will take their livestock to market on a bus. Instead of taking sheep, chickens and goats with them on public transport, the Dutch like to take their Bicycles, reading matter and at least one very large bunch of flowers for everyone to admire. You can buy a special ticket for your Bicycle. Reading matter and flowers go free of charge since (a) they bring so much joy to the passengers and (b) they are an excellent conversation piece.

Finally, the Dutch love to take dogs on all forms of public transport. Dog tickets are on sale if the dog is too large to fit in your shopping bag or prefers to sit on its own seat.

Rules for waiting for public transport

1. Whether you're waiting for the bus, tram, *metro* or train, as soon as it appears in the distance, form a compact mass with the others who are waiting. When it arrives, block the doors so the exiting passengers cannot leave. Above all, do not move out of the way when the doors open and people

attempt to get out, as this might speed things up. After all, you wouldn't want anyone to get ahead of you in the mob.

If, however, you are a passenger waiting to exit, then you have the right to curse the stupid idiots blocking your way.

2. In rush hour, there will be enough of you to form an additional blockade: stand or slowly stroll so as to prevent those who have managed to exit from hurrying to the stairs or escalator, or to a connecting bus or tram. In this "pinball" game, you score points each time someone bumps into you or is otherwise inconvenienced and frustrated by you.

On-Board Activities

If you want to blend into the local colour, be sure to passionately discuss the favorite topic of the country: guilders.

It is compulsory for Dutch nationals to complain, whine and express strong disapproval of food prices, subsidy levels, welfare benefits and the economy in general; but is highly inadvisable for non-Dutch to air negative views on Dutch ways.

If the train is waiting at a stop and it is quiet in the compartment, the mere rattling of a plastic bag is enough to draw the attention of all those within earshot. They'll immediately stop all present activities in order to try and see what you're going to pull out of the bag (and probably read whatever is written on the back of the bag).

Select your reading material to impress whoever happens to sit near you. It is obligatory that the person(s) sitting near you spend a considerable part of the journey studying your reading matter. Depending on their mood, they may do this while holding up their newspaper as if they are reading it, by casually glancing up from their book or by just blatantly staring. It keeps them happy — they are studying free of charge!

These days, you see people carrying computer books with pride, even though they probably have no interest in, and little understanding of, computers. Before the mid '80's, there was much resistance to computer technology among the Dutch. Consequently, computer books were frowned upon; indeed, the average *cloggy* wouldn't be caught dead with a computer book. If you were one of the few who did choose to read on that taboo topic, you would have done so at your own risk and certainly only if the seats near you were empty.

If you choose to write instead of read, their curiosity will double.

Behaviour

Rules of behavior on public transport are deeply ingrained in the Dutch. If you do not want to offend them, please observe the following:

1. If you are one of the first to enter the vehicle, spread your belongings out across the adjoining seat(s). Then stretch your legs out to block access to vacant seats. The rule is, sit in the aisle seat

when the window seat is not occupied. If someone comes along looking for a place to sit, ignore him/her by looking away, reading a newspaper or pretending to be asleep.

2. If the vehicle is full, you must stand inside the compartment where you are sure to block traffic when others want to pass through.

3. As a train approaches your destination, you must begin to fidget. If possible, stand up and fidget with your belongings.

4. Those in the back of the compartment must push, shove and/or stampede (it is tempting to say "queue" since the way in which they stand vaguely resembles a queue; but this is only because you must stand single file in the narrow compartment) to the front of the car.

Dutch law of motion:

"Exit time is inversely proportional to distance from door". In other words, those who sit nearest the door leave last. If you are in a hurry to get off the train, you must sit as far from the door as possible.

5. Upon arrival at glorious Amsterdam CS (Central Station), don't look anyone in the eye or

you'll be hustled — for hashish, heroin, cocaine, a cheap hotel or botel (boat-hotel behind station), sleep-in, left-wing newspaper, right-wing newspaper, non-affiliated newspaper, shoe shine, petition signing, joining in a demonstration or riot, recruiting squatters *(krakers)*, women's lib or gay lib. In any case, staring at the floor is good practice for the moment you exit the station and encounter the heaps of dog *shit* which decorate the streets of Amsterdam.

Take no offense to our use of the word *shit*. The Dutch have adopted it as an everyday word in their vocabulary.

Chapter 4

A DUTCH HOME

Ask a Dutch person about home and you will be told that it is *gezellig*, a word that they claim has no English equivalent. The dictionary translates it as "cosy". And, in this case, for "cosy" read "cramped".

The soul of the place is reflected through its living inhabitants – plants, pets and people – and the atmosphere *(sfeer)* is created by a widespread proliferation of inanimate objects. All these elements constitute *thuis* (home).

Urban Architecture

A typical old, urban house provides four separate accommodation units, or *flats*. There are two front entrances to the building, one for the ground floor resident(s) and one for the 2nd, 3rd and attic *(zolder)* residents. The very long and narrow staircase (see below) is found in the section leading to the upper storeys. Inevitably, one or more Bicycles hang from the wall above the bannister.

This efficient design provides:

- maximum inconvenience to those entering the building
- maximum disturbance to a resident hearing chattering, giggling, stomping locals enter or exit the building
- maximum inconvenience and disturbance to all concerned, by the uninitiated attempting self-disentanglement from The Bicycles (or trying to remove pedals, handlebars, etc. from an ear).

A curious architectural characteristic is located just below, or as part of the design of, the famous Dutch gable. A rusty old meathook hangs from a wooden or metal arm which extends from the front of the building. This is not a symbolic carry-over from the pacifist-nation's barbarous past. The hook supports a pulley which allows large, heavy items of furniture, and other bulky possessions, to be hoisted up from ground level. The windows and their frames are constructed for easy removal, thus allowing the load enough space for entry into the house on any floor. Many a Dutchman fears the public disgrace suffered if the load is allowed to adopt a pendulous motion, entering the building through a neighbouring window.

Other notable exterior features (optional) include:

- a short metal tube, extending from the front wall at a 45 degree angle. This is, in fact, a flagpole holder used to support the national flag on patriotic holidays. The ground floor installations are also used as litter bins and cigarette butt containers by urban youths.

- the spy mirror *(spionnetje)*, mounted on or close to a window frame. It resembles a large automobile "wing mirror" (probably stolen from a heavy goods vehicle) which older couples use to study street life, unobserved.
- a collection of old household junk, typically – gardening implements, toilet seat, washbasin etc. to add character to the abode
- a series of tree trunks extending from the nearest kerb to the upper-front wall of the building. These wooden megaliths serve to provide neighbourhood dogs with a natural toilet place, and to inconvenience pedestrians,

Subside-ized housing

cyclists and motorists alike. A secondary function is to stop the house from falling down.

- a human window cleaner, present and working, at approximately four-weekly intervals – irrespective of weather, time-of-year, or window conditions.

Stairs

This marvelous invention – the Dutch staircase – is called a **trap** or **trappenhuis**, and it is not uncommon to feel trapped when you climb the staircase. The **trap** will be steep and narrow, of meager depth (it will probably accommodate less than half your foot). In older houses, the staircase closely resembles a warped ladder.

Indeed, you must climb the stairs in the same way you climb a ladder, clinging precariously to the upper steps with your hands or to the bannister (if there is one), with one dangerous difference: there is no room for your foot to extend over the steps for balance, as with a ladder. The lofty Dutch accept this ridiculous arrangement as a fact of life; it provides that essential exercise that other nations obtain from climbing hills.

Following the path of the stairs, a rope or heavy cord passes through a series of loops and runs from attic to ground floor, terminating in a series of indescribable knots attaching it to the street door latch. This high-tech device allows residents of all floors to open the street door to visitors without the necessity of negotiating the stairs, which would entail more exercise than is good for a *cloggy* (too much stair-exercise causes untold wear on shoes and floor/stair covering, resulting in premature replacement of both!). Whatever you do, DO NOT use the rope as a bannister when ascending the staircase. You will trip the door mechanism and will be obliged to return to the front door again to close it. Continued misuse will draw you into an almost perpetual-motion situation, cycling between climbing up the stairs, climbing down the stairs, closing the door, climbing up the stairs . . . .

Furnishings

The favourite furniture styles are either pseudo-futuristic (Scandinavian influence) or imitation classical (German influence). Rooms are literally cluttered with the stuff, adding to the sense of claustrophobia already caused by:

- the lack-of-size of the dwelling
- the regulation Dutch color scheme, consisting of insipid shades of curdled cream and excreta brown
- the over-abundance of houseplants (see Chapter 5).

One area must be dominated by a desk and cumbersome bookshelves. With these two items present, certain tax advantages can be gained. The content of the bookshelves displays the image the owner wants to project.

Curtains are important in Dutch life. Almost every home has a double set of curtains: net curtains *(vitrage)* and heavier, full-length curtains. It is customary to leave the front-room curtains open day and night so everyone can look in and admire the possessions. Even the poorest of the Dutch get their hands on enough money to make their front room a showpiece, to give it their special *cloggy* atmosphere they feel is worth displaying to all passers-by. By true Dutch standards (see Chapter 8), the concept of paying for curtains by the metre, and only enjoying a quarter of them is heresy! Upon further reflection, it seems highly likely that the "unused" width is in fact used to mask the emptiness from thieves, vagabonds and squatters *(krakers)* when the official dwellers are on vacation, or otherwise not *thuis*.

The Toilet

Nowhere is the sense of claustrophobia more pronounced than in the water-closet. The Dutch have taken the term literally, and made that most private of rooms the size of a cupboard. Once you've managed to get inside the thing, you then face the problem of turning around to close the door and adjust your clothing. Before seating yourself, you face the dilemma of deciding whether you want your knees pressed tightly against the door or rammed under your chin. Any sense of relief on completion of your duties is counteracted by the realization that you must now find a way to manoeuvre yourself up and out again.

By far the most distressing feature of the Dutch WC is the toilet itself. The bowl is uniquely shaped to include a plateau, well above the normal water level. Its purpose becomes obvious the first time you see (or use) one. Why the worldy, cultured Dutch have this sadistic desire to study the recent content of their stomach remains a mystery. Perhaps it is not the sight of the deposit fermenting on the "inspection shelf", but the personal aroma that emanates from the depths and lingers in the closet for hours after the offending substance has been launched on its final journey.

The flushing system is a technological wonder. Not so much a miracle of hydraulic genius, but more a case of "find-the-flusher". The Dutch seem to derive some form of sadistic pleasure in constructing the most bewildering launching mechanisms. Be prepared for any of the following:

- a button on the pipe leading to a high cistern
- a button at the front of a low cistern
- a button at the top of a low cistern
- a lever at the side
- a chain, rope, or length of string
- a foot pedal
- a fish whose tail needs wagging
- a little boy whose tail needs wagging
- a linear motion, vertical action, flapper-valve actuating device: i.e., "knob" – that needs pulling.

If you don't find one of these, check for a spring-loaded pipe extending from the bowl to the cistern. If you find one, pump it — don't worry about your hand getting wet; it's all part of the game. If nothing works, return to your original location and complain about unhealthy people clogging up the works! Under normal circumstances, it's good sport; however, combined with the aforementioned aromatic horrors of the venue . . . enough said!

Whatever happens, don't pull the pipe extending from the front of a high cistern. This is an overflow pipe which will christen you with a large quantity of unblessed water for the duration of your occupancy. Even if it dripped on you earlier, please don't break it off now!

Typical W.C. decor consists of a birthday calendar affixed to the door; the compulsory plant (heaven help it); reading matter; a can of ineffective air freshener; and an aged, corny sign or cartoon requesting men to lift the seat.

The Kitchen

Second place for the smallest-room award goes to the kitchen, if indeed a separate room exists for it. This room, or area, epitomizes the Dutch gift for efficient space utilization. In lower income homes, the whole area is cluttered with cooking pots, utensils, houseplants and beer crates. An aging, white four-ring gas burner *(gasstel)* sits atop the refrigerator. In higher income homes, the whole area is bedecked with modern appliances (microwave oven, blender, juicer, food processor, etc), houseplants and beer crates. A stainless steel or brown four-ring *gasstel* sits proudly atop the smallest refrigerator.

No Dutch kitchen would be complete without the coffee corner *(koffiehoek)*, a sacrosanct area. displaying a drip-type coffee maker *(koffiezetmachine)*, an array of jars and cans, an abundant supply of condensed milk *(koffiemelk)* and a collection of coffee cups, saucers and miscellaneous dwarf spoons. A package of coffee filters is loosely pinned to the wall.

A small gas water heater *(geyser)* is usually mounted on the wall, above the sink, and provides hot water for the entire home. This configuration works well, provided only one hot water outlet is used at a time. If you take a shower and the water turns cold, it is probably because someone is filling a kettle in the kitchen.

Housepets

Favourite pets *(huisdieren)* include:

- cats (to catch mice)
- dogs (the smaller the abode, the larger the dog)
- fish (observation of which supposedly curbs violence)
- rabbits (for the children to cuddle)
- rats (to carry about town on owner's shoulder)
- exotic birds (to feel sorry for, locked in their cages).

A popular pet in country homes is the female goat, an ethnic symbol, to provide milk and cheese *(geitemelk, geitekaas)*.

Houseboats

There are around 2400 houseboats *(huisboten)* in Amsterdam alone. They are ideal living places for those who find the average Dutch house or *flat* too spacious. A houseboat is usually a shabby converted canal barge which provides one or two cheap accommodation units. In general, canal boats have no rusty hook hanging from a gable; the *trappenhuis* is replaced by an unstable, narrow gangplank; furnishings remain typical but fewer due to weight and structural limitations; the toilet cupboard is even smaller; raw sewage empties directly into the canal in which the boat sits. Ventilation is generally poor, heating is by means of an oil-fired stove, and cooking is done on a butane or natural gas hob. All this makes the habitat

a potential floating-bomb, and a houseboat home on a busy waterway adds a whole new meaning to the word hangover!

Despite these minor inconveniences, it remains fashionable to reside in a houseboat. Perhaps this stems from nautical traditions. Perhaps it's a means of temporary escape from the surrounding brick and concrete. In any case, houseboat living is "ethnic". Even though most houseboats have been permanently retired from their conventional roles and never go anywhere, the owners tend to work incessantly to keep the propulsion system in pristine condition.

In Utrecht, the red-light district basically consists of a row of houseboats.

Chapter 5

A GROWING CONCERN

Flower Power

If you want to express thanks, gratitude or sympathy to a *cloggy*, give flowers (**bloemen**, pronounced "blue men"). If you would like to apologize or patch up a quarrel, resort to flowers. If you are invited to dinner at a Dutch home, be sure to arrive bearing flowers.

The Dutch offer flowers to each other on all sorts of occasions. Where some nationalities would send a greeting card or others would arrive with a gift or other token, the Dutch say it with flowers. A *cloggy* on a Bicycle with a large bunch of flowers is as symptomatic as a Frenchman carrying a long, thin loaf of bread.

Bunches of **bloemen** should ideally be carried petal-down, in order for the excess water (from their previous abode) to leak through the wrapping and run down your sleeve. Whatever the event, unwrap the bunch upon presenting it to your hosts. They will transform before your eyes, as the very essence of their *cloggy*-being is reflected in an expression of ephemeral euphoria on their faces. A flower-rehabilitation and -grooming ceremony will take place before you are invited to join them in their humble dwelling.

When you enter a Dutch home, be sure to take a machete with you to hack your way through the growth. The Dutch are proud of their obsession with plants and flowers to the extent that the average living room resembles more a sub-tropical jungle than European living quarters.

When you finally find a place to sit, your gaze will undoubtedly fall upon additional vases of freshly cut flowers, prominently and strategically enshrined in highly visible locations. Further growth is nurtured just outside

the windows, in both the front and back gardens where available, or, in *flats*, on the window ledges or balconies.

Guilder Builder

Needless to say, the flower industry thrives, and therefore is a major source of revenue for the country. In parts of the remaining countryside, flower fields resemble a colourful patchwork quilt. Colder months and temperamental genuses are no obstacle to the industry, thanks to greenhouses.

In towns and cities, flower shops, stalls and barrows are abundant — with prices to suit every pocket. Holland is the largest exporter of cut flowers in the world. The flowers are sold daily to vendors at a large flower auction in Aalsmeer. The method used is the democratic "Dutch auction" (called "Chinese auction" by the Dutch) whereby the sellers bring the price down until someone makes the first bid.

Horticultural hysteria is not the exclusive domain of petals. Anything green and growing is a certain money-spinner. Plants for home use and vegetables for export also command a large space in the fields and markets.

Acquiring a budding new family member is only the start. Plant paraphernalia (an ornate pot, special soil, humidity gauge, various types of plant foods, leaf shine, etc.) is purchased/upgraded, without a great deal of thought for the purse. Whenever necessary, the household horticultural library expands with DIY books such as *Caring For Your Favorite Hevea Brasiliensis* and *1001 First Names for Your New Euphorbia Pulcherrima.*

It is yet to occur to the Dutch that all this growing of flowers and houseplants wastes good soil that could otherwise be used to grow crops. The crops could be sent to the starving masses in Africa, a popular subject for more protests in Holland (Chapter 11 — The National Passion). The world now waits with bated breath for the Dutch to protest this abuse of their assets.

Flowers for the masses

Ground Rules

One may think that incessant production of tulips, trees, tomatoes, turnips and 'taters would have rendered Dutch soil almost barren by now. Indeed not; for the regular application of cow crap and other fertilizing agents have kept their hallowed ground rich, right up until recently, that is.

Fields are becoming polluted with the residue from the 95 tons of manure, annually donated by the 17 million cows and pigs (four-legged variety) that inhabit Holland. There's just too much *shit* there.

Eager to capitalize on the prospect of florins for free faeces, provincial authorities have set up "manure banks" for deposit and withdrawal of the stinky stuff. To guarantee success, bank charges are levied on all transactions, and the whole nonsense is government subsidized. The latest word is that the *shit* banks are becoming a nationalized industry " . . . to promote efficient use of the surplus."

Timber Talk

In keeping with their love of plant-life, the Dutch have elevated the tree to almost "national symbol" status. Cities and villages provide generous budgets for the care and maintenance of trees. Each public tree is logged, numbered and carefully monitored. Tree doctors study, examine and perform surgery when necessary. The only form of tree-abuse tolerated is that executed by another over-protected species — *cloggy* kids (see Chapter 6), who happily maim, disfigure and mutilate the vegetation whilst experiencing freedom and union with nature.

Having said this, we now encounter a choice double standard of *clogism*. On the one hand, they export forestloads of wooden shoes around the world, as a symbol of their country. On the other hand, they are fed up with the stereotype image of the wooden shoe/windmill. A typical example of this conflict manifested itself while we were originally preparing this book. A Dutch illustrator pleaded to know:

> *"What kind of tune will the book whistle? Is it a book showing all Dutch people walking on wooden shoes, making porno pictures of their children for selling in the USA?"*

In this ecologically-consious, save-the-planet, celebrate-earth-day world, one wonders if the process of "extinctionating" forests in order to preserve wooden shoe/windmill table lamps, etc. is really valid, or whether the Dutch should re-think their strategy here.

A Dutch Dendro-paramedic

Chapter 6

CHILDREN

In 20 years I have never seen a child physically punished.

Luca Dosi Delfini,
Dutch art historian,
National Geographic, 1986.

There are two basic ways to bring up *cloggy* kids: the old, traditional way by teaching them some manners and respect (rarely found these days, usually only in what's left of the countryside) and the contemporary way as free, rude, spoiled, pampered gods.

Kid Kreation

Holland is a great place to go through pregnancy and childbirth, as every Dutch parent will tell you. Midwives and physicians undergo thorough obstetric training and practice. Natural births are encouraged in most cases, and home is considered the best place to do it. Wherever the baby-falling (*bevalling*) takes place, a mystical atmosphere of cosiness and intimacy prevails between all present. Strangely, no fresh-cut flowers can attend. When the newborn finally arrives, it is treated with utmost respect and care – perhaps too much so . . .

Raising Modern Dutches and Duchesses

The golden rule is: let them be free. Free to explore and experience whatever they please. Free to be "creative" (destructive), with little or no concern for others, as long as they are not in serious danger. They must learn to be independent and rebellious, as young as possible.

Speak to the little terrors in baby language until they finish their childhood (around the age of thirty).

In public, adopt an aire of strict(ish) discipline by giving instructions regarding behaviour that is permitted, and that which is not. Angelface will immediately disobey by testing the validity of a not-permitted aspect, whereupon cherub's activities are ignored.

Dat mag NIET .....

Typical Behaviour Patterns

If you visit a Dutch family, abandon all hope of being able to hold a reasonable conversation. A loud-mouthed child will inevitably:

- Place itself between host(ess) and guest, where it will dance (sometimes on your feet) and chatter to get attention.
- Cuddle up to mother, stroke her face and hair, or wriggle around in her lap, continuously asking stupid and unnecessary questions.
- Sit between you both, stare at you, and imitate your every facial expression and movement.

When the mother notices you are about to leave because of her sweet child's behaviour, she will tell the child, in her sternest voice, to go away and "let mama talk". The child will ignore her until the command has been repeated at least three times. Within five minutes, the child will return. The mother will be delighted to have her free, little angel back (totally forgiven and welcome to continue its previous activities).

Other favourite antics for Dutch children are to yell, scream, fight, cry, run around the room, climb all over the furniture, slam doors, bump into you, etc, again making it impossible to converse.

This attitude of parent and child continues in public: waiting rooms, transport, schools, on the streets, in shops and in restaurants. Above all, beware of the cinema syndrome where the combined traits of the adult, adolescent and infant *cloggies* merge into three hours of sheer hell (see Chapter 7).

Two mothers board a metro train, along with five small children. One of the children places her dirty hands on a gentleman passenger's bag. He tells her to stop. The mother, very shocked at the man's behaviour, explains (at great length) the importance of freedom for little children.

As she continues defending her child, the metro arrives at a station, the doors open, and one of the children steps from the train. The doors close and the train pulls away. As it is about to enter the tunnel, the woman notices the child is missing and pulls the emergency lever.

The recently-rebuked passenger smiles and remarks, "But the child was only being free . . . !"

As mother and five-year-old child walk past a display of kitchen units, the child heads for the units. Mother says, "Don't touch the cupboard doors, don't touch the cupboard drawers." The child continues towards the display. Mother says, "Don't touch".

Child arrives at display. Mother walks past the display on her way out of the shop saying, "Hey! Hallo!" Child opens and closes doors and drawers a number of times as mother does nothing to discipline her child for disobeying her, satisfied that the adorable child is free to touch and experience the cupboards.

In a supermarket, as mother is paying for food, child spots 10-cent plastic bags hanging by counter. Child helps itself to a bag. No reaction from mother. Child carries bag to mother and says, "Mama, I have a bag for you." Mother says, "That's not allowed" (the popular **dat mag niet**). Child ignores mother and mother ignores child. As mother packs her food away, child again offers her the bag. Mother says, "That's not allowed. **Those cost pennies! That's why mama brought her own bag.**" Child ignores mother, clutching bag. Mother advises that she cannot keep the bag. Child begins to cry and eventually drops bag in a heap on the floor. Mother and screaming child walk away. Bag is left on the floor. No attempt is made by mother to pick/hang it up again.

Matériel

Throughout the period of infantile pampering, training aids are strategically introduced. The first, a ball, is presented before the art of walking has been mastered. The second, The Bicycle, is introduced shortly thereafter (by the age of three, most mini-Netherlanders can ride a two-wheel bike competently). Next comes mother's greatest gift (to herself and to the child): kindergarten. This can start anywhere between the age of 30 months and five years. Also during this period, children are awarded their first pair of ice skates, which are renewed annually.

The school years that follow shape their worldly views. Parents may select the school(s) their offspring attend. The choices available are based on classical education, philosophy and religion. Nowadays, classical education teaches the children to be "streetwise". Education based on philosophy is for *avant-garde* parents and has its roots buried in freedom of expression (with obvious results). Selection of a Christian school enables parents to segregate their children from Turks, Moroccans, etc. (who follow the Muslim faith) without being seen to be racist.

When full-time education is finally completed, the Dutch are suitably prepared for welfare or work – see Chapter 9. Parental pampering now diminishes, for the school-leavers are well versed in the art of babyhood.

Holland's Future

Twenty years on, the current herds of freeborn Dutch, with their divine qualities, will be the backbone of the country. They will be the mainstay of industry, the financiers and the polititians.

Dutch kids, spawned by over-liberated mothers and welfare-minded fathers, will rule and govern the country. They will be steering the ship. A classic case of *Dutch Helm Disease!*

Chapter 7

CINEMA

Cinema appeals to the Dutch. It is actively linked to the culture-vulture and individual-expression syndromes that all self-respecting Dutch persons acquire at birth. Unfortunately, their tenacity for over-respecting themselves, and under-respecting others, causes a total breakdown of consideration in the world of cinema. If you want to SEE AND HEAR a feature film in Holland, wait for the videocassette version to be released. If you merely wish to preview the decline and fall of civilization (as we know it), a Dutch cinema *(bioscoop)* is for you.

Behaviour

1. The number one rule is that you must giggle, chatter, belch and rattle your candy wrappers as much as possible, to ensure that no one can follow the film. If anyone's presence irritates you, throw your empty bottles and other rubbish at them while making loud and nasty comments about them.

2. If the theatre is not yet full, be sure to select a seat directly in front of someone else and to sit up as straight as possible (preferably with a tall hat on) so as to block their view. Better still, fidget frequently.

3. Make every effort to arrive late so as to inconvenience as many members of the audience as possible by blocking their view and stepping on their feet as you find a seat. If you have missed part of the film, ask the people sitting near you (in a loud voice) to explain in detail what has happened so far.

Intermission

The programme intermission provides a rest period for the audience. Join the stampede to the foyer for obligatory coffee (to ease the throats of the better behaved), soft drinks or beer (to massage the throats of the worst behaved) and for restocking munitions of wrapped confectionery, etc. The middle ranks will remain in the theatre, rehearsing for the return game. At the end of the intermission, smokers casually deposit still-smouldering cigarette ends in waste paper containers and all persons over 5ft 11in must delay returning to their seats until the programme has recommenced.

DO NOT even consider prematurely finishing a conversation to view the film.

Subtitles

When it comes to subtitles, the Dutch take the "sub" (meaning: *of inferior quality*) to heart, excelling in their usual manner.

Imported cinema presentations are shown in their native language with Dutch subtitles. Many are of U.K. or U.S. origin. Native English speakers are misguided if they believe that comparison of the spoken word with the written word will further their knowledge of the Dutch tongue. The following translation rules are used:

- Make basic errors, such as translating 96 as 69, or 1959 as 1995.
- When it comes to translating humour, you must destroy any chance of the audience understanding what is going on.
- Don't bother to translate words (spelled the same, but with a different meaning) such as "gift" (English = present; Dutch = poison) or "hare" (English = rabbit; Dutch = her).

Chapter 8

MONEY

(ON GULDEN POND)

"How do you take a census in Holland? Roll a dub-beltje along the street."
It has been said that ". . many a true word is spoken in jest . . .", and here is living proof.

The main unit of Dutch currency is The Guilder *(gulden)*, ridiculously abbreviated *HFl* or *f*. Higher denominations (ten guilders and up) are represented by inanely designed paper notes, printed in equally inane colours. Lower denominations consist of coins of various sizes, the smallest being the 10-cent piece *(dubbeltje)* which approximates the size of a shirt button. The largest denomination coin is the 5-guilder piece. It is not the currency itself that has prompted the inclusion of this Chapter, but the manner in which it is revered by its bearers.

Bargain Hunting

The Dutch enjoy spending time going to various shops, all over town, in order to take advantage of special offers and sales. They'll gladly spend an extra two hours shopping in order to save five cents on a can of beans. Some will even spend more on public transport than they save at the sale!

When shopping for clothes, they will search the racks and shelves, frantically looking for a slightly soiled or damaged article. This gives them licence to demand a price reduction. If they find one, they will purchase it whether it fits or not. It can always be used as a birthday present, or kept in storage for several years in case of weight gain or loss, or until their children grow into it.

In most of Europe, winter sales start in early January. In Holland, the sales begin towards the end of January. This eliminates the temptation for Dutch people to postpone Christmas until early January, thereby saving some of their precious pennies. January sales can be a violent experience in many countries. Risk the Dutch version at your peril.

All year round, sales and special offers abound, categorized as **uitverkoop** (sale); **aanbieding** and **aktie** (special offer); and **reclame** (advertised price, not to be confused with reclaimed land). None of these categories generate as much excitement as **alles moet weg!** (everything must go).

A maze of complex and confusing rules governs price reductions *(reductie)*. Foreigners would require the equivalent of a master's degree on the subject to begin to understand how to manipulate the system. The Dutch appear to be born with this ability. As an example of the extent of the problem, no fewer than 19 different types of reduction were listed in the national railway guide for 1985-86.

Street Markets

Every Dutch town or city has a deluge of street markets *(markt)*. Whether open daily or just once a week, regular attendance is compulsory for self-respecting *cloggies*. For tourists, this is the place to go to:

- have your wallet stolen (if you haven't already managed to do so on the tram)
- see everyday Dutchmen wearing their famous wooden foot-attire *(klompen)*
- buy drugs, stolen goods, cheap imitation antiques, and other rip-off merchandise
- experience the stench of rotting fish, vegetables and littered streets
- find yourself compacted among an endless throng of local tribespersons progressing at a snail's pace.

For local inhabitants, the street market is an exception to their rule of penurious shopping. They'll pay over the odds (to a limit) for the privilege of shopping at their favourite stalls, at their favourite market(s). The pilgrimage is not complete until they orate about the visit to their friends, neighbours, etc. This is also the one occasion where they refrain from bitching and whining about prices.

Second-hand Transactions

If you advertise the sale of second-hand items, you must expect to waste time over numerous long telephone calls probing for precise information on every imaginable detail about the *te koop* ("for sale") item(s). Even if the item has been sold, the callers will want to know all the details in order to know if they have missed a good bargain.

Getting the price you quoted is a difficult feat. We offer the following guidelines:

1. Compromise them before they compromise you. Upon entering your *flat*/home, the prospective buyer will take an instant mental inventory in order to select a conversation piece to steer the topic in his favour. The ensuing discussion is used to prepare you for the I-can't-afford-that-price speech.

2. Attitude. Adopt the firm attitude that the advertised price is the only acceptable price. Ignore arguments that the item can be purchased at a lower price at the local market. If that were the case, the prospective buyer would not have wasted his precious money and time on the phone call and journey.

3. Change Syndrome. Every good *cloggy* will arrive with money stragetically distributed about their person. If the quoted price was HFl 40- a successful transaction will unfold as follows:

- One pocket or compartment will contain HFl 30-, one will contain HFl 10- and one will contain a single note of HFl 100- or more
- Upon eventual agreement of the price (HFl 40-), the buyer will produce HFl 30- and rummage around to discover the HFl 100- note, assuming that you will not have change for the large note
- This would appear to be the crucial moment. Do you risk losing the sale if you maintain your price, or call his bluff?
- You call his bluff. After a further reluctant rummage, he will produce the crumpled HFl 10- note. You are happy to receive the full price. The buyer is content knowing that he gave you a good run for his money.

Shelling Out For Fuel

When the Dutch buy gasoline, they don't fill their tank; they buy in multiples of five litres. For each five litres you purchase, you get one savings stamp *(spaarzegel)*. To fill the tank regularly may result in the loss of two or three stamps over a few months! A full card of *spaarzegels* (approx. 40) can be cashed-in for the monetary equivalent of 3.33 litres of gasoline. Alternatively, one can elect to receive a special (read: trashy) gift.

Fines

Fines are fine for fine people. In Holland, an intricate system exists whereby the State levies fines encompassing such common misdemeaners as illegal entry and parking offenses.

When you see arriving passengers being interrogated by the police at Schiphol airport customs, you will probably assume they are drug dealers. Wrong. Chances are they forgot to pay a parking ticket during their last stay in Holland.

Pay your parking tickets if you ever plan to return to Holland! If you fail to pay a ticket, and attempt to enter the country at a later date, you run a high risk of being detained by the police at the port of entry. They will require you to pay for the ticket, even if it's years old, plus a fine.

The same applies if you inadvertently miss paying your last rubbish collection bill or if your residency permit expires while you are outside the country. When you try to

Pay your fines !

re-enter, you will likely be diverted to the 'explanation chamber'.

This restitution justifies the government's outlay on "high tech" equipment such as computers, multi-channel synthesized hand-held transceivers, etc.

Banks

In general, the banks are efficiently and professionally run. They would be. The Dutch would have it no other way.

Personal experience indicates that debit transactions are balanced on a daily basis while credits are acknowledged up to seven days after the fact.

Given the public's appreciation of orderly queuing, bank branches tend to issue numbered tickets when the complement of clients totals one or more. As a bonus, this system eliminates the possibility of labeling the bank undemocratic, sexist, racist or withdrawal-ist.

Bank cashiers can adopt as unhelpful an attitude as possible:

> Can I have a transfer form?
> *No.*
> Why?
> *We don't give out blank ones anymore.*

(At this point play them at their own game:)

> Can you type the information onto a blank one,
> and give me the form to take away?
> *Yes!*

Cashiers are most helpful in one respect: they happily share confidential banking information, such as your current bank balance, with all within earshot. Once again, Dutch openness prevails.

A Sporting Chance?

The Dutch love to be associated with sporting activities, provided the cost is not too high.

On a skiing vacation, they will insist (from the very first lesson) on zigzagging their way down the slopes. After all, they have paid for the journey to the top and must therefore extract maximum value from the journey down.

The laws of magnetism dictate that the Dutch will be attracted to mountain climbing. Having no such natural features, they improvise by climbing man-made vertical barriers, such as an underpass ret(r)aining wall near Amstel Station, Amsterdam. This activity, of course, is free of charge as the walls were erected for other purposes. It provides an authentic training ground; after all, everyone knows that 20th-century architecture strongly resembles the snow-encrusted peaks of the Alps and the Himalayas!

Football *(voetbal)* is the national sport. TV programmes are cancelled without warning to show matches. If their team wins the cup, the whole town gets drunk. If they lose, the whole town gets drunk.

Ice skating is another extremely popular sport, in large part due to the fact that anyone can skate for free on the numerous canals, ditches and other waterways.

When they fish, they religiously use two rods: Their fishing permit allows maximum two rods. Any fewer would be abusing their purse by not getting their money's worth.

Personal computers have evolved as an entertainment-cult throughout the western world. The Dutch finally succumbed to the passsion after years of characteristic resistance (Chapter 3), to the point of infatuation. Electronic libraries, known as Bulletin Boards, link dedicated users throughout the European and North American continents and beyond, by telephone, to individual libraries called Nodes. One of the most popular systems is "FidoNet", and its November 1987 listing of Bulletin Boards quoted:

W. Germany	Italy	Netherlands	U.K.
Pop. 60 million	Pop. 54.5 million	Pop. 14.6 million	Pop. 5.5 million
26 nodes	26 nodes	104 nodes	67 nodes

Perhaps the reason for the tremendous success of this sport in Holland is that Bulletin Boards invariably provide for the acquisition of information, programs, games, etc., free of charge. Thus immediately appealing to the mass of (potential) computer addicts.

At Times of Sadness

The most unsavoury aspect of the "Guilder Builder" characteristic manifests itself when tragedy strikes.

A Dutch funeral is an occasion where the Dutch excel at money-related cold-mindedness. A recently bereaved spouse or parent must be ever-cautious to the profiteering of funeral organizers. In the event that you are unfortunately placed in this position, recruit the aid of a *cloggy*. He/she will guard you against:

- Overpriced floral tributes (the usually cheap bouquet of flowers can cost 200-300% more when ordered for funeral purposes)
- Overpriced coffee (while your only thought is to lay your loved one to rest with dignity and respect, your aide will embark on a debate over

the funeral arranger's price-per-head for coffee and biscuits, compared with the local *café*)

- The futility of paying extra for piped music if you
  think nobody will be listening to it.

Afterwards the whole congregation adjourns to the
abode of the next-of-kin for a drunken and relentless
round of bickering and bartering over the spoils.

Chapter 9

UITKERING

(THE DUTCH WORK ETHIC)

We believe you must give people a basic wage, and let them choose whether or not to work.
                              Gerrit Jan Wolffensperger,
                              senior Amsterdam council member

---

If you truly want to integrate with Dutch society, you must have at least one type of *uitkering* (welfare, national assistance; pronounced "out-caring").

Applying for welfare, and reaping the benefits, is not a social disgrace – it is a right. (In 1986, one quarter of the population of Amsterdam was on welfare.) Those government employees whose role in life is to approve your *uitkering* will give you all the assistance you require, to the point of helping you re-write your application to receive maximum payment. If you don't qualify by answering *JA* (yes), then answer *NEEN* (no), the social worker will likely advise.

The System

Basically, there is one requirement to obtain your *uitkering*: you must be prepared to spend a long time in the dismal, unventilated waiting room(s) on numerous frustrating occasions.

Advantages of having an *uitkering* are as follows:

- It kills any incentive you may have had to work. This is excellent training for the Dutch youth.
- It gives the Dutch government an excuse to have one of the highest tax rates in the world.
- It attracts thousands of foreigners, especially Turks and Moroccans (so the Dutch can prove they aren't racist).
- It encourages those who get the urge to work to do so illegally (*zwart*, "black") to supplement their income.
- It encourages many to live abroad, on welfare benefits, at the expense of those who pay taxes.

Although Holland has one of the most comprehensive welfare systems and superior national health programs, and even though there is no true poverty in the country, the natives still voice their disapproval. They want more. And they want it free *(gratis)*. Many women, youths and foreigners rally behind the motto *Bijstand Mis$tand* (Welfare = $-Abuse). Others interpret *Bijstand Mis$tand* to indicate their opposition to welfare because it makes people dependent and therefore is a "capitalist slave-making system". The point here is that the Dutch themselves cannot agree on the meaning of the motto around which they rally.

Work Attitude

Despite the attraction of a more-than-adequate unemployment benefit, some choose to actually work for a living. The idea here is to impress your employer for a period of three months after which it is practically impossible for him to dismiss you, as will be seen later.

During the probationary period, you will no doubt experience some frustration regarding the lack of effort extended by your colleagues. Once you complete your three months, your working life takes on a completely different character. You belong.

You can now concentrate more on the "social aspects of work." Work now interrupts coffee breaks. A two-hour debate over the validity of your boss's order receives higher priority than the five-minute task of executing it. A colleague's birthday takes top priority. It allows various workers to arrange a collection, purchase celebration requisites and organize the compulsory "surprise" party. You, as birthday boy/girl *(jarige)*, are not left out as it is your duty to provide edible delights. The party, of course, takes place during company hours. It is left to the reader's discretion to fantasize the effects of (say) the Olympic Games in Holland!

Timekeeping is no longer a matter of conscience. Remember that the Dutch form of the expression "The early bird catches the worm" is:

**"The early bird is for
the cat."**

Dismissal – Failure or Success?

An employer must give you a "reasonable" (but un-specified) amount of verbal warnings as to your misconduct. Next, three written warnings must be issued (on separate occasions). These are only officially recognized if you (the accused) acknowledge acceptance in writing. Without your acceptance, the matter goes to arbitration.

With your signature, the case is presented to the local authorities for assessment, and possible authorized dismissal. The word "possible" is used here meaningfully. Should the authorities decide your dismissal is valid, your newfound unemployed status will inevitably qualify you for welfare. Welfare through unemployment is typically 70% of your last salary, paid by the same local authority (1988). Given the Dutch affinity to the guilder (Chapter 8), it follows that the local authority will be hesitant to approve a dismissal.

You can have quite a nice time working in Holland!

Subsidies

Generous subsidies of all types are available. The most common is the housing subsidy *(huursubsidie)*. Also widespread are educational grants and subsidies. These include the arts. Often the financial encouragements are in the form of a purchase of the subject matter by the government, in order to help the aspiring artists. The works are hung in a multitude of public buildings for all common taxpayers to savour. In 1973, a psychiatrist was subsidized to pose on a pedestal in a museum, proclaiming himself to be a work of art. (Hopefully he also was hung in a multitude of buildings.)

Life is based in large part around the amount and types of subsidies one receives. Recipients of welfare carefully weigh the financial consequences of starting part-time or full-time work. A job lowers or terminates their welfare and subsidies.

A work of art?

Time-Off

Every individual recognized by the social security system, employed or otherwise, bank president or street sweeper, is entitled to 25 days holiday *(vakantie)* each year. This may seem overly generous until you consider that a large part of the holiday pay *(vakantiegeld)* is deducted from the individual's wages throughout the year and paid back during the holiday period together with the employer's contribution, after taxation. Thus the thrifty Dutch award about four weeks' holiday and pay for roughly half – a classic example of "going Dutch". Again, it is the **uitkering**-ites who win, as they receive a bonus with their welfare payments for four weeks of the year.

Sick leave is yet another way to maximize an employee's welfare benefits. When you report an illness, representatives are sent to your home about once a week to "confirm" that you are at home and are genuinely ill. The visits are only allowed to take place during specified hours (Monday to Friday, mornings until 10 and afternoons from 12 to 2:30) of the first three weeks of your illness.

This procedure rightly allows the critically ill sufficient latitude to shop for the necessities of life, such as flowers and coffee, without the fear of losing any welfare entitlement.

Chapter 10

MET WIE?

(IDENTIFICATION & PHONE HABITS)

Official Documents

If you spend more than a few days in Holland you will undoubtedly be baffled by the Dutch obsession with paraffin (misspelled, *parafen*). Indeed the word appears on most Dutch documents.

A Dutch *paraaf* (signing of initials) consists of one or more large, illegible scribbles, used mainly to ensure that no one but the originator can decipher the initials. The formal signature *(handtekening,* lit. "handdrawing") is equally as enigmatic as the initials, only there is more of it. Whether using the *paraaf* or handdrawing, the process of bold and daring scribbling provides positive identification of the Dutch nationality.

Of equal importance on some documents is the **stempel** (rubber stamp). While some documents require only a **paraaf**, others need the handdrawing and yet others need the "stamp". Sometimes a combination of stamp + paraaf, or stamp + handdrawing, are called for.

Place and Date

Other vital ingredients of a legal Dutch document include the date and place *(datum en plaats)*, despite the fact that the place can easily be falsified and is inconsequential.

I.D.-ology (proof of identification)

When the Dutch bark *"legitimatie"* at you, for once they are not being rude; they are not probing into your family history or parentage. The word is harmless, meaning "identification".

The Dutch alien residence card *(verblijfskaart)*, issued to non-Dutch dwellers legally residing in the Netherlands, requires strong proof of identity and purpose for its issuance. Yet this card is not considered a form of identification by most institutions, including the post office, even though it bears your name, photo, handdrawing, birthdate, place of birth, nationality and alien registration number, verified by minimum two **stempels** and an official handdrawing by an authorized member of the alien police. Additional space is provided on the card for

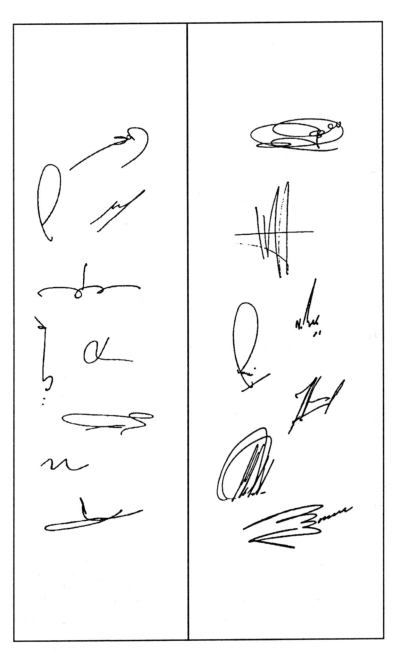

Dutch Paraffin   Handdrawings

"notes", each of which is duly stamped, dated and initialed by an officer.

Introductions

When meeting a Dutch person for the first time, a mutual monotone mumbling of names takes place. Expressions such as, "How do you do?" "Pleased to meet you," etc. are not used. During the introduction, your gaze should be a vacant one. Avoid eye contact.

Hand contact, called "hand giving" *(hand geven)*, consists of a nervous, damp, limp hand-wobble (see Chapter 14). The facial expression is one of boredom and indifference.

Telephone Manners

In Holland, you must state your name every time you answer your phone. If you fail to do so, the other party will either lapse into silence or demand to know who you are *(met wie spreek ik?)* before uttering another word. *Cloggies* are seemingly incapable of holding any type of telephone conversation without knowing your name:

- "Can I speak to Mr. van Doorn?"
- *"What is your name?"*
- "John Smith."
- *Bluntly, "Ja!*
The switchboard is closed.
Call back later."
- "Can I leave my name or a message?"
- *"No!"*

Many Dutch suffer from telephonophobia *(telefoonvrees)*. The symptoms include anxiety and extreme nervousness when dealing with both incoming and outgoing calls. The Dutch are at a loss to explain the origin of their phone fear, but admit that it is not unknown for the weak-hearted to go into cardiac arrest at the sound of a ringing telephone.

Perhaps one cause of their telephonophobia is that deep in the subconscious mind, they all know what to expect when dealing with calls to or from a business, public office, etc . . . If you try to obtain a piece of information, you get passed from one number to another. After four or five frustrating calls, each time repeating your name and request, you are fortunate if you reach the correct office.

If you do not know the toadstool (*toestel* or extension number) or department *(afdeling)*, it will be necessary to explain in great detail to the switchboard operator why you are calling, and why you are calling them. Just as you reach the interesting part of your lengthy explanation, the operator, not knowing what on earth you are talking about, will either:

- Cut you off
  or,
- Connect you to a toadstool, seemingly selected at random. When someone answers, you must begin your explanation all over again . . . . and again . . . . and again . . . .

When you ring the police, expect to have a long wait until someone replies. Offer the burglar or murderer in your home a cup of coffee to stall him while you wait for the police to answer your call.

In order to lessen the trauma of the general population over their phobia, plush public telephone booths are placed at convenient locations throughout the country. These structures are not so much provided for the purpose of making telephone calls, but for the therapeutic exercise of hypervandalism. By daylight, the telephone directory can be destroyed and replaced with graffiti — written and sprayed from floor to roof, inside and out. When darkness descends, and the general public have had time to read the graffiti, all windows and other breakable components (including the apparatus itself) can be destroyed. On weekends, the booth can be set on fire.

Chapter 11

THE NATIONAL PASSION

This is a self-regulatory society; it is not governed by speeches from above. We allow as many people as possible to be themselves. Some call that anarchy; we call it civilization.

Klaas de Vries,
Socialist Member of
(Dutch) Parliament

The (Dutch) urge to be original often leads to utter nonsense....

Han Lammers,
Queen's Commissioner for
Flevoland Province, 1987.

The Dutch love to devote time to a "good cause". They express their devotion in the form of demonstrations, riots, debate and the inevitable collections. The common denominator is protest . . . .

When these gentle pacifists are inconvenienced or their egos ruffled, they instinctively resort to aggression and/or violence of tongue and deed. They get their way. More so than any other nation. But it's never enough for them. They always find more to complain and protest about. This perpetual cycle of confrontation and inherent change has been instrumental in reducing excesses of the wealthy and powerful. Consequently, class distinction is minimal. The philosophy would appear to be:

- We hate anybody telling us what to do.
- Speak out! (At times the government and law enforcement agencies are paralysed by the thought: "People would not stand for it.")
- Defy defiance.

Defiance is found even in the isolated areas with rigid rules and strict moral discipline. In 1971 in the village of Staphorst, where polio vaccination is forbidden, most parents had their children inoculated during a polio epidemic.

A favourite method of self-expression is the use of "profound" slogans/maxims. These are often presented in the form of pathetically unsubtle jingles, such as *"woning, geen kroning"* (housing, not coronation) on the occasion of the coronation of Queen Beatrix in 1980, or *"wonen niet spelen"* (housing, not games), when Amsterdam was a candidate for the 1992 Olympic Games. Such sayings are proudly displayed in various ways:

- Graffiti. Graffiti is used as a means of bringing the message to the masses. It can be found in abundance at places where the public gather. Main transport termini, church walls and surviving telephone booths are popular bulletin boards.

- Buttons. Featuring the established slogan/maxim for the cause, handwritten and often including a crude cartoon-like illustration or motif. These are conspicuously displayed on the clothing of sympathizers and supporters of the cause as medals of service. It is not uncommon for the chest of the enlightened bearer to be adorned with a multitude of different campaign buttons, thereby giving indication of rank to the protesting legions.
- Stickers. Designed much as the buttons, but somewhat less abundant, probably due to the relatively high cost of production.

A Slogan-sticker: "I do it with (a condom)"

- Banners. These are usually made from old bed sheets and house paint and are erected or hung from the rooftop or windows of a protester's home or headquarters on the day of the official protest. Thereafter the device is left in place to rot, as a symbol of freedom and remembrance to all disinterested parties.
- Promotional T-shirts. These tend to incorporate more patronizing phraseology, such as those used to promote the 1992 Amsterdam Olympics with the slogan: "Holland wants the world to win."

The tide began to change in the late 1980's when some groups decided that slogans "don't work anymore". Instead, these groups elect to write and analyse thorough annual reports, in order to impress politicians and the police.

Complain, Protest, Object, Appeal

Disagreement in Holland is voiced through the accepted channels of **Complaint, Protest, Objection** and **Appeal**.

When the Dutch disagree with something, the first step is to **Complain. Complain** to anyone who will listen. Grumbling and complaining are part of the Dutch way of life.

Having found sympathetic ears, the next step is to **Protest.** With the support of the ears and their associated mouths, the **Protest** can be made known to the offending party. This is usually accomplished through the medium of the written word.

Only when the **Protest** is met with overwhelming apathy does the disagreement gain momentum. The sympathetic ears and mouths now become an offended action *(aktie)* group, and the disagreement automatically enters the **Objection** phase. This phase is an overzealous form of the **Protest** and can include pleas, threats, demands and anything else that would likely win the day. The more determined objectors arrange for their dispute to be included in specialist community publications.

The final conflict is manifested as the **Appeal**. To win it requires all the support and cunning a Dutch(wo)man can muster. The **Appeal** is a battle of wits and manoeuvring in both written and verbal form (when a Dutch neighbour was once asked for advice about a dispute, she advised, *"Je moet nu een grote mond opzetten"* – lit., "Now you have to open your mouth wide").

Appealing, Dutch Style

This four-element procedure is followed at all levels, official and unofficial, domestic and bureaucratic. It is valid in the case of an inconsiderate neighbour. Equally, most official letters dealing with government finances end with a clause stating that YOU HAVE THE RIGHT to ob-ject *(bezwaar indienen)* to the government's decision. Even the Dutch tax form states, "After some time you will receive a reply to your letter of objection. If you do not agree with this reply, you can appeal." You usually have one to two months to appeal. Depending on the cir-cumstances, your letter can be sent to the office in ques-tion, to the mayor or to the Queen.

Causes

The causes, protests and incessant gum-bashing about "opinion" are all done in the name of freedom and the Dutch concept of democracy. As soon as the suffix *–vrij* (free) is added to a noun depicting a supposed evil force, the word is sanctified and warrants flagrant public display. Thus *"kernwapenvrije gemeente"* (nuclear weapon-free community), *"rookvrij gebouw"* (non-smoking building).

Although the Dutch will scrimp and save every last cent, morsel of food or scrap of clothing whenever pos-sible, they do like to give, but only to what they consider to be a worthwhile cause. This is usually through an or-ganized foundation *(stichting)* with tax-free status.

A *"Fund for Relief from Persecution and Euthanasia of Amphi-erotic, One-legged Mice in the Southern Province of Western Zildenavia"* would give the Dutch pride in their worldly consideration. Such a cause will be supported as totally justified as it encompasses the following (Dutch readers please note that the order presented is alphabeti-cal, and in no way politically or emotionally prejudiced):

- Gay-rights
- Handicapped-rights
- Lesbian-rights
- Rodent-rights
- Trend factor (popular in the 70's and 80's were "we hate America(ns)", anti-nuclear all, euthanasia, etc.)
- Unfamiliar location/ethnic-rights.

This cause will warrant demonstrations, riots and, most important of all, collections. Donations will inevitably be void of taxation.

The logic behind the attitude is described in promotional material from an Utrecht *aktie*-group:

**"Actions, in which and
through which,
people are offered the
opportunity to take
action themselves."**

Any legal resident of Holland may hold a demonstration. It is their democratic right. Whether it is supported by five or 50,000, it is allowed to take place. Demonstrations must be well-organized and co-ordinated with the local authorities. Every town or city has its own rules for this activity. Specifically, you must inform the local police of the intended date, time and especially the goal of the event, after which you will be advised of any necessary modifications to:

- Date and Time, which will be changed if previously-approved demonstrations or civic events conflict with your plans.
- Route, which will be changed or streets closed to traffic depending on the anticipated support for the cause.

When all is agreed, you receive your demonstration permit and the necessary preparations can be made for the day. During the demonstration, you will naturally experience increased police presence. Do not be dismayed. They are individuals first and policemen second. Some will even display your campaign button on their uniform.

Non-approved demonstrations are not permitted, but are often allowed if they are orderly and do not disturb traffic — and depending on the appearance of the protesters and the general acceptance of the goal.

"The Dutch Way"

The most successful of Dutch causes are elevated to the rank of "The Dutch Way". The Dutch Way is an audulation bestowed upon those principles and prejudices that command the support of 250% of the population. In this respect, housing rights command the prime example. Long-suffering parents are anxious for their post-pubic offspring to vacate the nest while the *enfants terribles* themselves cannot wait to feather their own nests. But there are no empty homes.

The Dutch answer to this situation, of course, is to form pressure groups, known to the outside world as *krakers* (squatters). The *krakers* fanatically oppose the acquisition of empty buildings for speculation. They believe that all reasonable and uninhabited space should be translated into subsidized housing for them. This is The Dutch Way.

Krakers invade vacant places: office blocks, individual flats, shops, warehouses, any dwelling which is vacant for more than a few days. The *krakers* cause came to a head during violent riots in Amsterdam in the 1970's. The police were forced to call in the army, which brought in a tank to move the crowd. The confrontation ended only when the city agreed to renovate the occupied building for the squatters. *"We have the squatters under control now..."* A city housing official summed it up by stating that the job would cost more than a million guilders, "an expensive way to deal with a little social unrest. But it's the Dutch Way."

Women's Lib

Women's lib is probably the most extreme example of the "National Passion" that readily demonstrates, sorry, exemplifies . . . itself. And no wonder! The Dutch government willingly provide 12-13 million guilders annually for feminists to do "research". The modern Dutch *Vrouwen* (women) are so fanatical about their genetic characteristics that they elevate femininity to the highest pinnacle possible. They are WOMEN. And people, humans, etc, secondly. *Vrouwen* have their own *cafés*, their own magazines, books, newspapers, theatres, travel agencies, union, and of course, their own therapy centres. Through these media, *Vrouwen* can, and do, form pressure groups which effect radical changes to society and its laws, on such subjects as birth control, abortion, divorce, homosexuality and equality-through-dominance.

Vrouwen-causes are a classic and typical obsession for the modern Dutch to identify with. Any variety can trigger a chain-reaction with the hope of achieving the ultimate goal of a Europe-wide demonstration against things that ordinary people would class as petty fads.

As an indication of the severity of the infliction, the 1987 Amsterdam Telephone Directory listed no less than 27 entries under *"Vrouwen"* alone. Amongst the more paranoid were:

- *Vrouwen Actiecomité van Vervroegd AOW-Pens.*
  (Women's action committee for early old-age pensions)
- *Stichting Aktiekomitée Vrouwen in de Bijstand*
  (Women's welfare action committee foundation)
- *De Vrouwenfietsenmakerij*
  (Women's Bicycle Repairer)
- *Vrouwenklussenkollektief de Karweiven*
  (Women's Odd-Jobs Collective – the "Female Odd-Jobs")
- *Internationaal Archief vd Vrouwenbeweging*
  (International Archives of women's movements) who boast 45,000 volumes (mostly in Dutch) of gender-related information.

While gathering background material for this Chapter, in mid-1988, we attempted to contact 33 women's organizations in order to ascertain just what they were for. Of the 33 enquiries dispatched:

- 20 were never replied to.
- 3 were returned, unopened.
- 9 replied enclosing details of their craft, and promotional brochures, obligatory stickers, etc.
- 1 replied by postcard, demanding to know "*. . . who you are, how you got our address, where you learned dutch and what you are going to do with the information . . . .* " !!!

So much for the feminists' desire to make their suffering known to the whole of man- and woman-kind.

Typical of the confused mentality reflected in the replies we did receive: "*. . . we are not against anything. We demand the right to live according to the custom of this country, and not to be seen as half of a couple but as an individual person and be treated as such.*" . . .

Domestic Bliss — *à la Vrouw*

**...... the custom of the
country being that
man goes to work,
WOMAN remains
home with children
and housework.**

Finally on this topic, an extract from a pamphlet supplement issued by the Amsterdam Migrant's Center. The extract is included here in its original, unabridged English language form:

> *". . . And a last example, in which the center did not play a role: Amsterdam house wives became a lot more critical on the quality of the vegetables on market places having noticed how the Surinam, Turkish and Moroccan migrants make their choise. The daily supply of previously unknown vegetables proves the influence of the new cuisines on Dutch cooking."*

(Answers on a postcard, please, to . . . . . .)

Military Service

Dutch military service is limited to a 14-month period for young males. To some it is no more inconvenient than a stay in a holiday camp. The ranks are permitted to retain long hair, earrings and other symbols of their mid-childhood, and enjoy full labour benefits (controlled working hours, public holidays, etc). Even the officers have a union contract. Gays are welcome at all entry levels, as an inquiry in the early 1970's found homosexual exclusion to be discriminatory.

The military deterrant

Yet still the protest-happy Dutch feel a need to herd together as an expression of their rights to freedom and individuality. At present, the alternative to military service is to become a conscientious objector, officially recognized and categorized. A *dienst weigeraar* (service refuser) can perform civilian-type work, or a *totaal weigeraar* (complete refuser) can lounge around in a military prison for about two years.

The debate continues; there are continuous discussions about shortening the length of service and about exemptions for religion, study, etc.

Women are accepted in the services on a volunteer basis only, and are often ridiculed by the general public.

Presumably, some are protesting for the right of compulsory service, or refusal; basically . . . . . .

**. . . to have the right
to go to prison for not
wanting to do
something they are
currently not required
to do!**

Chapter 12

RULES FOR SHOPPING

The Dutch love to window shop and to browse while dreaming of the ultimate bargain. Perhaps in fear of relenting to sales-pressure, many also suffer from the bizarre affliction known as **drempelvrees** (threshold phobia — fear of entering shops, restaurants, etc.). Having managed to cross the **drempel**, they revert to type. For your own protection, take heed of the following:

General

1. For smokers, before entering a shop, find a waste bin containing dry, combustible material to throw your burning cigarette in.

2. When entering stores, let the door slam in the face of the person behind you. If you hear a loud thump or bang caused by a person in a cast, a pram or a wheelchair, nonchalantly turn around

and mumble, *"Surrey whore"* (see Chapter 16). If you're in a particularly benevolent mood, you can further announce that you didn't notice the person's cast or wheelchair.

3. If someone gets in your way, place your hands on his/her shoulders and impatiently push the person aside, as you show off your French, uttering ***"Pardon"***.

4. If your purchases amount to less than HFl 20- and a queue of more than three people is formed behind you, pay by cheque or credit card and take at least five minutes to search for your identification. Alternatively, delay the transaction, using whatever means possible, until the queue has extended to eight people.

5. Hunt for bargains and complain about prices of ALL produce/merchandise — see also Chapter 8.

In Supermarkets

1. Take a few one-guilder pieces as deposit for use of a trolley. Until 1988/89 the peel-off, ring-tab from a beer or soft drink can was considered by much of the population to be legal tender for this purpose.

2. If a *cloggy* offers you an empty trolley in exchange for a guilder, beware! Either the mechanism for refunding your guilder is broken, or the wheels malfunction.

3. Frequently block isles with trolley.

4.   Recruit kids to covertly load other shoppers' trolleys with expensive items.

5.   At the checkout, the cashier must make two announcements: ***dag!*** and ***zegels? Dag*** means "good-day" and ***zegels*** means "savings stamps". The latter is NOT a gutteral ***Sieg Heil***, as many Germans have learned to their cost.

6.   Check egg cartons for quantity and condition of contents. Usually, at least one egg will be broken or missing. Note also the "Dutch Dozen": 1/2 dozen = 6; 1 dozen = 10.

7.   Prod and poke delicate items. When about to leave, complain to the shop assistant about the poor quality of the produce.

Shopping For Clothes

1.   When visiting fashion shops, take ear defenders with you to avoid permanent ear damage from the compulsory disco music blaring incessently therein.

2.   If you notice someone searching through a full rack of clothes, stand nearby and push the clothing apart so that you close the gap the person had made.

3.   Take your children and encourage them to play hide-and-seek amongst garment rails.

At Street And Flea Markets

1. If you see an item you wish to buy, show minimal interest in it. Tell the vendor you saw the same thing for less than half the price at another stall, in order to launch into a healthy bartering session.

2. If a crowd has gathered around a particular stall, push into the crowd, dig your elbows into those in front of you and breathe heavily in their ears to give them the hint to move out of your way. Conversely, if you are in the front row of a crowd studying the display of a stall and others try to elbow their way in, hold the fort. Do not leave until the crowd has dissipated.

3. When the market is extremely busy, walk against the flow of traffic, stopping frequently for no particular purpose.

Chapter 13

DRIVING

As with shopping (Chapter 12), a first experience of driving in Holland can be positively bewildering. But do not be dismayed. You are not an inferior driver. You have simply missed some elementary un-written rules of the road.

Freewheeling Ways

1. Drive as close to the car in front of you as possible.

2. Change lanes constantly while driving. Roads are built from taxpayers' money. If you've paid your taxes, it's your right to use as much of your road as possible.

3. At least two cars should go through each red light. Avoid, at all cost, reducing speed or stopping. Any brake-light indication combined with an amber or recently red traffic signal will subject you to a barrage of stereophonic horn-blasting.

WARNING! Beware of elderly drivers. They stubbornly adhere to the old-fashioned system of preparing to stop when the lights turn amber, and religiously stop at red lights. These senior citizens are the cause of many collisions.

4. If you witness a motorist driving through a red light, sound your horn violently, in tribute, while you visually scold the violator for his flagrant disrespect of the law.

Move alongside him and pound your head with your right hand. Appropriate angry facial expressions, bouncing up and down on your seat, and yelling **idioot!** (idiot), **godverdomme!** (damn it) and **klootzak!** (scrotum) are beneficial. Never mind the fact that you are more of a traffic hazard than he was as you accelerate, slow down and wander across the fast lane, concentrating on your gesticulating.

5. If you are the first car to stop at a red light, do not expect to be able to see the traffic lights (thanks to brilliant Dutch engineering, your car will be sitting directly under the lights). Just relax and rely on a honk or two from the car(s) behind you. Horns are guaranteed to sound if you do not react instantly to the green light.

Alternatively, step out of your car until the light changes. This, at best, is taken as a form of Protest by the locals, and at worse is taken as an expression of your individuality. Both earn you much respect.

Road Rights

Dutch democracy on the roads is exemplified by inconsistent yield signs, well-described by the saying,

"Sometimes the small roads have to have the power."

There would appear to be no general rule, such as "priority to the right" or "priority to the main road."

Consider roundabouts as an example. In some places, the car coming from the right has the right of way. In other places, the car on the roundabout has the right of way. Elsewhere, traffic lights are used.

As local respect for speed limits is non-existent, popular means to slow down the traffic in residential areas include one-way streets and **drempels** (berms, or speed bumps).

Getting Your Licence

There are two ways to obtain a Dutch licence: by taking lessons through an authorized driving school or by surrendering a valid foreign licence for a Dutch one.

Not not all foreign licences can be surrendered for a Dutch licence. Until the 1970's, most foreign licences were acceptable. Many Dutch would go to, for example, Egypt to obtain their licence. The total cost of the trip (including the licence) was less than the Dutch driving school fees. In other words, the *cloggies* got a free trip to Egypt while obtaining their licence.

Now a recognized foreign licence cannot be traded for a Dutch one unless the bearer can prove that he/she lived or worked in the foreign country for at least six months.

The driving school is rigorous and expensive (about HFl 2,000- to prepare you for your first driving test). All sorts of interesting and unique equipment is used; some classrooms provide individual steering wheels and gear levers for the simulation phase. Do not be discouraged if you fail several driving tests; each additional course will only cost you roughly half as much again.

Strangely, the high cost of driving lessons has not been affected by Protest (Chapter 11).

Chapter 14

ON
DUTCH CUSTOMS

*All hail the Dutch, long-suffering neutrons in the end-
less movement against oppression and exploitation.
Let us hear it for the Dutch, bland and obliging victims of innumerable wars which have rendered their
land as flat as their treats ... Every one of them is an
uncle, not a one can muster real courage ... All hail
the Dutch, nonpeople in the people's war!*

Tony Hendra,
National Lampoon, 1976

Non-Racist Nation

The Dutch boast that they are a non-racist nation. In
the 60's, they were extremely proud of the lack of
prejudice and racial problems in Holland. But there was a
reason for this situation: non-caucasians were a rarity in
Holland in those days. The result was that darker-skinned
people were idolized by the Dutch.

Things changed when Dutch Guiana became the independent Republic of Surinam in 1975, and hoards of Surinamese flooded the country. The crime rate, drug abuse and number of people on welfare increased phenomenally. Immigration procedures soon tightened for dark-skinned applicants, hence, "We support your cause, we appreciate your dilemma; but don't want you here!" Or, in the words of Dr. H. G. Boswijk, an Amsterdam clergyman, *"When Surinamers come to our churches, people observe a friendly distance. They say, You are welcome but leave us alone. It's a kind of implicit apartheid."*

Yet, as soon as a residence visa has been issued, the Surinamese and other dark-complexioned immigrants (such as Turks and Moroccans) become a welcome part of the Dutch heart-throb, for they are now THEIR ethnic minority. In addition, they are on equal footing with the locals since they are eligible for welfare benefits.

And mankind must SEE that Holland leads the world in acceptance of other races in a western state. This attitude is demonstrated in the current policy of recruitment for the police force. One goal was to have a force consisting of 25% women and 10% minorities by 1990. In order to achieve this, a policy was established for Dutch citizenship to be granted in six months, instead of ten years, to successful applicants.

To further fertilize their insistence that they are inherently non-racist, several government (and other) offices provide information and brochures in Moroccan and Turkish, where none exist in neighbouring European languages. Hot-lines are also available. This is one of Holland's great contributions to the European Community.

Manners Maketh Man

Little can be said about Dutch manners. *Cloggies* firmly believe their manners are impeccable, but to an aware foreigner they are as rare as a dike-mender's drill.

When abroad, *cloggies* assume no one they meet will speak Dutch. They ridicule others by making sarcastic and derogatory comments about them in Dutch. Occasionally they find themselves ridiculing fellow *cloggies*. No embarrassment or bad feeling ensues as:

- both parties realise that they are guilty of the same.
- on discovery of their common nationality, both parties will agree that the ridicule is justifiably applied to the intended alien targets.

At home or abroad, a Dutch greeting consists of a brief handshake in the case of new acquaintances, or of a kiss on each cheek for longer-term friends. Whichever form of greeting is used, it is often accompanied by a feeling of dread, as it gives rise to yet another national phobia: the fear of sweaty hands *(zweethanden)*.

Camping

Camping is a popular recreational pursuit. It is easy in Holland — official campgrounds are havens of comfort, with hot showers, shops, etc. Individual sites are marked, pre-planned by the owner, and there are obviously no "rough spots" on hillsides, etc.

Almost every household owns a camping shelter of some description. It can be a 1-2 person ridge tent, a grand family tent with awning and rooms, a caravan or a trailer. Yet not all are used for overnight accommodation. For some curious reason, *cloggies* make a habit of erecting tents in public parks for a few hours during a sunny day (the practice is quaintly called "day camping"). It may take 2-3 hours to travel, pitch the tent(s) and arrange the accessories (collapsible chairs for seating, table for the coffee paraphernalia, plant pots and/or flowers, etc.) for a mere 45 minutes relaxing with nature; but they do it. *En masse.*

At home or abroad, overnight public camp sites are an excellent place for the young *cloggies* to sadistically impose their freedom on others. Around dawn, the little ones like to begin to sing Dutch children's songs; for a while, their parents will not interfere with this exercise of freedom and national pride.

When the songs finally get on the parents' nerves, they gently tell their little darlings to hush. The children exercise perfect disobedience and carry on singing and shouting. Those *cloggy* children who do not like to sing can find freedom of expression by talking in an obnoxiously loud voice.

Older children (up to 30 years of age) have their rights to freedom, too, and often express themselves by playing football through the campsite. Other great places for the kiddies to play football are restaurants, *cafés*, full car parks, golf courses and *metro* trains.

Another favourite pastime is cussing and breaking (various types of) wind. Making fun of others is, of course, a must, accompanied by lots of very loud giggling and cackling.

Sign Language

To become an accepted member of Dutch society, we recommend you practice the following, preferably in private:

- Place hand parallel to ear, 3" from ear. Oscillate hand in a forward/aft direction at medium speed. This means "delicious" *(lekker)*.
- Double thumbs-up with lateral pumping action from the elbows whilst religiously chanting *"Omsterdom!!"* This means, "I like where I live."
- Spread fingers, palms uppermost, and extend forearms. Tilt head to one side as you emit a sound not unlike a sick cow: *Jaaaaa.* This means, "I don't really believe you."

See Chapter 13 for special sign language when driving.

On Marriage

A popular contemporary attitude of unmarried couples living together *(samen wonen)* is that they should have the same rights as married couples. If the boyfriend's father dies, his partner feels entitled to two days' paid holiday for the occasion, as is the case for married couples.

Living-apart-together is commonplace as it allows couples to have their own life most of the time, but also to be together and have a shared non-binding commitment. Above all, there are tax and welfare benefits . . .

For couples who do elect to marry, the obligatory Town Hall ceremony (church ceremonies are supplementary and optional) clearly defines the extent to which the partnership is to be taken . . .

Money under matrimony is Money shared.

The controversial topic of clergy and wedlock has been understandably fierce in Holland. The attitude is summed up in a BBC television interview with a Dutch theological student in the 1970's:

Q: *How do you feel about the idea of a priest being able to marry"*
A: *No question at all. It's a question of the priest himself, and not of other people. When I want to be a priest and I want to be married; and the Pope, he wants a priest (who) is not married; I don't want to be a priest!*

Get the idea? More on the consequences later.

Women's liberation has drastically modified the accepted format of a marriage. Dutch women, with their overstretched sense of fair play, have achieved what they see as a "more equal division of labour" through the practice of partial or total role reversal. The authorities indicate their approval by awarding the major tax concessions to the higher income partner – male or female – rather than the traditional method of assuming the man is the family "breadwinner".

The Coffee Cult

Cloggies run on coffee. They can exist on over-boiled potatoes and cabbage, but they run on coffee. Fresh Dutch coffee; grown in Africa and South America, but roasted and packed in Holland. Custom-built vending machines brew it and discard the unsold liquid at timed intervals. The armed forces take it on NATO manoeuvres in thermos flasks. Businessmen and truck drivers alike *en route* to other European countries gorge themselves with it before crossing the border, and complain bitterly about foreign coffee, drinking as little as possible for the duration of their trip. Many shops, including supermarkets, lure customers with free coffee. At main railway stations and in intercity trains, vendors patrol the platforms and corridors with coffee carts.

In all fairness, Dutch coffee far excels its dishwater-style cousins, served in the U.K. and U.S.A. It is strong and distinctive in flavour. In keeping with this endowment, for years the populance were treated to an annual coffee-rating contest, sponsored by the well known magazine/publishing house of Elsevier. Each year, different blends were tasted, by experts, in order to establish the cream of the drop, in the same way that France, Germany and Spain rate their wines.

The Netherlanders' method of drinking Dutch coffee is an art in itself:

1. Check all necessary components are present: cup of piping hot coffee; dwarf-sized spoon or stirring stick; condensed or powdered milk; and sugar.

2. Support cup in one hand. If a saucer is provided, do not hold the cup, but grip the saucer as if it were a frisbee about to be thrown.

3. Add milk to cup to colour (optional).

4. Add sugar to cup to taste (optional).

5. Stir continuously until cool enough to drink. If you use sugar cubes, pound the lump until dissolved, then stir vigorously for the remainder of the cooling period. If you added milk and/or granulated sugar, alternate between clockwise and counterclockwise stirring. If you drink your coffee black, stir however you choose. The important thing is to stare hypnotically into the cup while you stir.

6. Remove stirring implement from cup. Tap wet end 2-4 times on the rim of the cup. This indicates to your colleagues that you have completed the stirring phase and are about to enter the drinking phase.

7. Return stirring implement to cup.

8. Hold cup with fingers and thumb diametrically opposed (If a saucer is present, do not use the hand holding the frisbee). If the cup has a handle, insert middle two fingers through the handle. Extend the index finger up-

wards and across the cup to clamp the stirring implement against the far end of the cup. This is important as it prevents the implement from entering your nose in step 9.

9. Raise cup to mouth and slurp loudly while drinking. After first slurp, announce *"lekkere koffie, hoor!"*

The Other Cult

The Dutch possess a proven respect for religion. Traditionally, the country is divided between the catholic and protestant faiths (reference books are contradictory about the exact ratio: apparently even the Dutch can't agree upon what they are!); whatever the divide, it is modified to roughly 100:1 for the customary sport of:

POPE-BASHING

The origins of this appear to be the archaic policies of the Vatican in respect to contraception, abortion, divorce, clerical celibacy, and acceptance of homosexuality, not to mention, of course, women's ordination (**vrouwen** priests). In short: fucking and females.

Irrespective of centuries of papal politics and policies, the blame for everything is placed firmly on the shoulders of Pope John Paul II.

It all came to a head in May 1985, when Public Enemy No. 1 visited Holland as part of his altar-stop tour. The warm welcome provided by the Netherlands consisted mainly of street riots, demonstrations, protest pop songs (**Popie Jopie** was the best selling record), satirical comedy in schools and on national television, etc. The regiment of slogan writers originated such absolute gems as **POPE GO ROME**; **PAUS RAUS** (get out, Pope!); **PAUS ROT OP!** (piss-off, Pope!); and . . . . . .

The following Sunday, the Dutch were back in their catholic churches, praising the Lord. No large queues were evident at the confession boxes.

There was no shame or embarrassment. No one, Royalty or commoner, condemned the rioting, and Prime Minister Lubbers reflected, "The Pope came here as a man higher than others. That is not the Dutch way."

Festive Occasions

Queen's official birthday. This is celebrated 30 April (birthday of her mother) when there is some chance of dry weather, since the ruling monarch's true birthday is in January when the weather is guaranteed to be inclement. Many cities turn into a large flea market for the occasion. The Dutch save up their old junk and try desperately to sell it on this day. There are infinite street stalls selling all types of food and beverage, spread throughout the town centre. The crowds are as unbearable as the overpopulated bars. There are flower parades, jazz and rock 'n roll bands, magicians, school marching bands, and other forms of entertainment.

Two Christmasses. On 21st November, the Dutch Santa Claus *(Sinterklaas)* travels from Spain to Amsterdam, by ship. After clearing port customs (parking fines, excess toys, etc.), he is often greeted by the Queen before stocking-up with drugs. Santa has a white beard, wears a long red robe and tall red/gold hat, and carries a golden crook. He is attended by his black manservant Peter *(Zwarte Piet)*, provided the former can prove that Peter is not his slave, and the latter can provide evidence that his presence is only temporary and dependent upon Santa's acceptance.

The Dutch celebrate Christmas on December 5th and again on Christmas Day/boxing day. There are two Christmasses in order to split the material one (gifts) from the spiritual. Gifts are exchanged on the 5th. At night, children place their shoes by the fireplace. The shoes are filled with surprises from Santa during the night, which partly explains why Netherlanders have such big feet.

New Year's Eve. As this is the only time fireworks are allowed, it must follow that the Dutch New Year's eve lasts from 15 December to 15 February. Or do they celebrate *Blitzkrieg* during this period? Your first experience of New Year's Eve in Holland may give the distinct impression that the country has gone to war. It is dangerous to walk about town after 10 pm as the *cloggies* love to throw exploding firecrackers at passers-by. This form of entertainment continues throughout the night. Bars and restaurants close at 8 pm and open again around 11 pm or midnight. Public transport stops at around 8 pm.

Liberation Day. Traditionally, liberation day celebrates the freeing of the country from its Teutonic military oppressors in 1945. Celebrations are now confined to 5-yearly bashes due to prohibitive costs. In actual fact, the *Reichmark* has been replaced by the *Deuschmark*, soldiers have become tourists, and once again Wagner is more popular than . . . .

National Windmill Day. National Windmill Day is not observed nationally. Of all the areas that do observe it, most do so in May. Presumably, most of the "most" have windmills.

Chapter 15

BIKES, DIKES, FLAGS & FAGS

This chapter focusses on some traditional and contemporary things for which the Dutch have received a measure of global recognition. The list is understandably short, and is headed by the tourist money-spinners windmills and tulips — both of which occur and recur in other chapters of this work. Here we include **Bikes** (in honour of Dutch perseverence with the infernal machines); **dikes** (those all-important irrigation features, without which this book would be a collection of blank pages); royalty and patriotism (those ancient traditions that the Dutch simultaneously love and hate, typified by the the practice of flying **flags** at every slightest excuse); and homosexuals (colloquially referred to in English-speaking countries as **fags**).

Bikes

There are more than 580,000 of them in Amsterdam alone. Whether this only counts roadworthy vehicles or includes the mangled, decimated lumps of rusty no-wheelers chained to bridges and lampposts throughout the city is unclear. What is clear, however, is that the Dutch are so fond of them, that around 85% of the population buy them! They come in various shapes, sizes, and vintage; irrespective of which, they are all dearly loved and respected. There is a thriving black market industry in them, and facilities for spares and repairs are almost as plentiful as dog*shit* on the pavements.

They are called *fiets*, probably because that's what powers them. Their drivers are Kings/Queens of the Road (Queen Juliana would ride one to the local street market) whose wanton disregard for other road-users encourages them to career from kerb to kerb, up to four-abreast.

Public buildings, parking facilities and public service vehicles are all designed with the two-wheeled wonders in mind. Most major roads (except highways) include a personal lane for them. Whenever and wherever possible, this lane is a separate thoroughfare, complete with its own roadsigns and traffic lights.

These magnificent machines are used in many roles: as personal limousine, goods vehicle, freight wagon and taxi, thanks mainly to a twisted tubular steel accessory — the carrier. The carrier carries crates, kids, cats and canines alike (special child seats can be installed at the front and rear of the frame, for larger families). In the absence of these household items, it provides a rear seat for one or more passengers (traditionally the girlfriend,

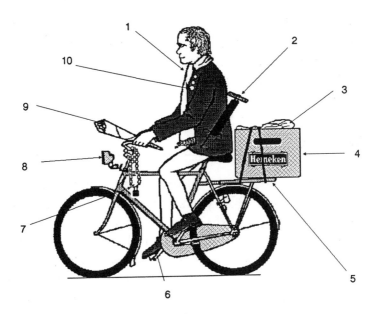

1   HAND-KNITTED (OR PLO-STYLE) SCARF

2   STIRRUP PUMP (NOT TO BE LEFT ON BIKE)

3   PLASTIC CARRIER BAG (SUPERMARKET OR BOOKSHOP ISSUE).
    MAY ALSO BE CARRIED ON HANDLEBARS

4   TYPICAL CARGO

5   REAR SEAT/FREIGHT COMPARTMENT — MAX. LOAD 250 LB (112 KG)

6   SIZE 10 EMERGENCY BRAKING SYSTEM (2-CHANNEL)

7   ANTI-THEFT DEVICE. MAY ALSO BE WORN AROUND NECK,
    OR WRAPPED AROUND SADDLE SUPPORT, IF PREFERRED

8   DYNAMO-DRIVEN HEADLIGHT (PREF-ERABLY DENTED) —
    SHOULD NOT WORK

9   BUNCH OF DUTCHNESS

10 COLLECTION OF "BUTTONS" WITH TOPICAL MOTIFS (PEACE, LOVE,
    ANTI-NUCLEAR NONSENSE, ETC)

Nedlanderthal Man

boyfriend, wife or husband, or any combination of these). Heavier cargo (pianos, cupboards, etc) require the borrowing/rental/purchase of a **bakfiets**, a sturdy *fiets* modified to incorporate a large wooden box or platform at the front.

Dikes

The Dutch have been building dikes, dams, ducts and ditches for about 800 years; and they still need more. They've been seriously messin' about with water for longer; and they've still got plenty left. They've tried to blow it away with windmills, pump it away with windmills, convert it to paper and flour with windmills; and have created a tourist industry in the process. The product of their labours is called the Dutch "landscape": a subaqueous plain, or (almost) dried-up seabed.

A typical *cloggy* stands some 18½ hands high (6ft 2in or 1.88m) — noticeably taller than the global average. In the event of a natural disaster, they can act as human periscopes and view their country as it was before man bespoiled it.

Perhaps due to their inability to tame the raging waters, they have become experts and innovators of waterways and bridges. They have partitioned an area of the North Sea, formerly known as the **Zuiderzee**, into a freshwater lake and are currently reclaiming large areas of this. A motorway runs across the partition *(afsluitdijk)*. The southern delta region (prone to periodic flooding) has been harnessed by a series of hydraulic dams. None of this could have been achieved without serious protest, debate, demonstrations and compromise.

In 1958, Parliament made positive moves to protect the country against flood disasters as a response to public disquiet following the devastating floods of 1953. In the late 60's, protests were voiced about the project. The completion date of the last and most complicated part of the project was set for 1978. This was delayed due to protest and debate focussing on the barriers being "normally open" (to maintain the natural environment) or "normally closed" (to ensure the safety of the population at all times). In other words: plankton vs. people. Complete closure, for which contracts had already been awarded, was out of the question. The compromise called for the barrier to be kept open in normal circumstances, but to be closed during heavy storms. All-in-all, the project was delayed some eight years and cost 30% more than estimated, with HM Queen Beatrix officially opening the storm surge barrier in October 1986.

Ever eager to profit from their talents, the Dutch have exported H2O control technology to the extent of creating picturesque coastal landscapes in countries where a barren interface previously existed.

Back on the domestic front, the remaining water does have its uses. A primary mode of industrial transportation is the canal. Barges are more commonplace than articulated vehicles. In mid-wintertime, when the water becomes ice for a few weeks, nothing is wasted. Ice skates are donned by all from 2 to 102 years of age for a season of free travel — for leisure, business, sports and fitness.

Flags

With true originality, the national flag is the French *tricolore* turned sideways. That is: blue under white under red. It is displayed at every excuse by the patriotic. The post-war period has seen the Dutch strive for a unified Europe. During this phase, patriotism declined and fewer and fewer flags flew. With this goal supposedly a reality from 1992, Dutch fervour has refocussed on fear of losing their identity. Flag manufacturers are predicting record sales in the ensuing years.

National events with royal connections are differentiated by the addition of a 4-feet long strip of toilet paper, stained orange. Holland is one of the few European countries which still retains a monarchy as a figurehead — with its inherent scandals and obscene levels of personal wealth. (The Dutch royal family is among the most wealthy in the world.) The Orange-Nassau family's most recent claim to fame involved Prince Bernhard — husband of the recently-retired royal favourite Queen Juliana. Not content to live in luxury courtesy of the Dutch purse, he enjoyed the fruits of favour "donated" by American defence firms in order to enhance the quality of their products. As a result of this scandal, the ever popular Queen Juliana, in true Dutch fashion, threatened instant abdication if her husband were subjected to the embarrassment of a public trial. After an "investigation", the government agreed to drop the matter providing the Prince resign from all official duties.

Not wishing to be outdone in the protest stakes, the Current Couple set the scene for their inauguration by establishing a link with the German Nazi era through associations with the *Hitlerjugend* and the *Wehrmacht*.

Love prevailed, and Claus von Amsberg became the prince consort of the Netherlands. At the regal betrothal (1966) some one thousand *cloggies* violently demonstrated, shouting **"Claus, raus!"** (Claus, get out!). It took 17 years for the Dutch to accept this latest Teutonic invasion, and then only so after he suffered and recovered from a mental breakdown.

As a further indication of Dutch latent belief in the divine rights of royalty, all goods deposited on the streets is officially the property of the crown. If on royal-rubbish collection day your neatly bundled waste has not been removed, but stands solitary at the entrance to your abode, the reason must be that either:

- Their Majesties have sufficient stocks of rotting kitchen waste, etc, to last until next collection day.
- You have been officially honoured by the crown, who have decreed that you may keep that week's tribute as a royal bequest.

However, you have some possibilities concerning the immediate problem . . .

1. Leave the rubbish where it is.
- City authorities will not notice your rubbish amongst the scattered heaps of monarchial mess.
- The neighbours, however, will. They will probably write you a nasty note or come to your home and complain about their Queen's garbage you left on the street. Children, dogs,

cats, birds and vermin will rip the sack open and spread the contents about (reaction from neighbours as above).
- Rural authorities will notice your rubbish and will most likely take action against you.

2. Remove the rubbish to a skip, a rubbish heap or another street where the palace has yet to make its collection. In cities, no one will care in the least. However, it is only fair to warn you that in the country, civil servants are a bored species and will inevitably search through the container(s), looking for clues of ownership. If the bag contains any items which include your name and address, you can expect to receive a photocopy of the evidence, along with a warning *(waarschuwing)*. After a second warning, you'll be reported to the police and/or fined, presumably for stockpiling stolen goods.

Oversize rubbish can be abandoned on city streets on collection day and will be collected by a special service. Oversize-rubbish-eve and -day provide a fascinating view of Holland: the streets are decorated with items such as refrigerators, stoves, washing machines, pianos and furniture.

In towns or villages, the local authorities are far more respectful of their Queen's property. You can make an appointment to have oversize rubbish collected once a fortnight. Bear this in mind on the day you buy your Christmas tree, as you should, on the same day, make an appointment to have it hauled away a few weeks later.

Fags (and Fagettes)

Gay boys and gay men (*flikkers*) came out of the closet in the 60's. The discovery of the fact that there were other *flikkers* about, fired by their inherent (Dutch) rebelliousness and permissiveness, led to the formation of *aktie* groups, followed by demonstrations, gay rights movements, gay centres, gay bars, hotlines and periodicals.

The inevitable reaction of *Vrouwen* homosexual movements took place soon thereafter, with lesbians demanding equal rights and more-than-equal facilities. At least one lesbian couple has had a child through artificial insemination and was last reported to be receiving generous welfare benefits.

Despite their common homosexual *raison d'être*, gays and lesbians are separate entities. In general, women are marginally accepted in gay bars while men are more taboo in lesbian bars and *cafés*. One area of commonality is that of self-glorification. The aptly-named newspaper **"De GAY Krant"**, in August 1988, listed gay and lesbian facilities in approximately 100 Dutch cities, towns and villages, including 180 entries for Amsterdam alone.

Amsterdam's liberal locals constructed the world's first monument to homosexuals in 1987 — an obvious structure in the form of three large triangles, painted pink. Soon after, work started on a portable *homomonument* which was presented to the British Government as a protest against proposed anti-homosexual legislation there. The rest of the population strives to be extra "open" and accepting of homosexuals, bisexuals and portable monuments.

Chapter 16

THE DUTCH LANGUAGE

Like most nationalities, the Dutch insist that their tongue is a difficult one. Dutch is basically a form of German which borrows heavily from English and French, although most native speakers will vehemently deny this. If you speak German, you will have an easy time with Dutch. From a grammatical viewpoint, it is easier than German.

Dutch is rarely encountered abroad. Basically, there is no need for it outside of the country. Conversely, if you spend more than half a year in Holland without learning the language, your Dutch acquaintances will appear offended that you haven't learned their wonderful language.

If you take a course in the Dutch language and finally progress enough to dare to utter some sentences in public, the person you speak to will inevitably answer you in what they detect to be your native European tongue.

They love to show off the fact that they have learned one or more other languages.

The more you try to learn Dutch, the more the Dutch refuse to speak Dutch to you and the more they complain that you haven't learned it.

The abundant use of many vowels (including double vowels) as well as the construction of long words (as in German) give the written language the appearance of being difficult. However, Dutch is very regular in its pronounciation and grammar.

Throat Disease (Pronounciation)

There are only a few difficult sounds: the gutturals (represented by the letters *"sch"* and sometimes by *"g"*); the *ui, ij* or *ei;* and the single versus double *"a" (man, maan).* If you have never encountered the language but are tempted to experiment with these examples, try reciting the list of ingredients from a soup can, with your mouth half-full of syrup.

During World War II, the military's secret test of the Dutch nationality was to have an individual pronounce the name of the town of *Scheveningen* (pronouned Shave-a-Nigger).

It takes some time for outsiders to grow accustomed to the sight and sound of the native's names, as they are long and numerous. Although you will probably be asked to use a one-syllable, vowel-happy forename (Huub, Jaap, Peet), the birth name is invariably a formal one, followed by 1-5 middle names and a surname. In the case of married women, the maiden name is attached with a hyphen. Examples . . .

Peter Johannes Theodorus Gustav Arnoldus De Jong

Hubertus Cornelis Johann Maria Van Dijk

Wilma H. J. M. D. Van Leeuwen-Waterdrinker

Basically, the official combinations rarely appear anywhere except on larger legal documents, for obvious reasons.

It is extremely difficult to have one's name changed in the country, usually only by royal permission. The only exception is if the name is embarrassing!

Grammar

There are two genders: neuter and a combined masculine/feminine. The masculine-feminine merge (or noun lib) happened years before gay and women's lib.

Nowadays there are three forms of "you": *U*: polite and formal; used in business and with elders. The use of this form of "you" shows respect. *U* is used less and less these days. If its use deteriorates in proportion to the national lack of respect, it will soon be extinct. Either *jij* or *je* can be used for the singular familiar form; *jullie* is the plural form (not a girl's name).

The character of a people is reflected in its language. An example of this is seen in the compulsive-obsessive use of diminutives in daily speech. As a Dutch physician explains, *"Everything has to bear the stamp of the small-scale complacency, which personally I consider to be one of our most typical features."*

The suffix *-je* is the most common way to exercise this. The Dutch drink *een kopje thee* (a little cup of tea), take little strolls (*gaan een straatje om*) and take little journeys around the world (*reisje om de wereld*).

Trend Setters

hallo
Don't let what appears to be friendliness fool you when you first arrive in Holland. When someone says *hallo* to you, this is most likely not a greeting, but rather, an explicit expression of contempt, to draw your attention to something stupid you have done. It is used to embarrass (generally, this is most effective with non-Netherlanders).

sorry
Common form of lip service, often used in combination with "whore", as in "Surrey whore" *(sorry, hoor)*.

SVP
The French "silver plate" (spelled *s'il vous plaît*) is often used in its abbreviated form, *SVP*, on signs and in letters, as a replacement for its direct Dutch equivalent *AUB* (in full, *als 't u blieft*), or "(if you) please".

Spelling Corruptions

Much of the population likes to use modern or progressive spellings which are not yet official, such as **buro** for **bureau** or **Odeklonje** for **eau de cologne**. The latter also exemplifies the battle between traditionalists, who prefer to leave *"c"* as *"c"*, and those who consider themselves progressive, preferring to replace a hard *"c"* with *"k"*. The results of this struggle are resolved in some dictionaries by a blanket statement "If not found here, look under "c" ("k").

Intrinsic Idioms

met de hakken over de sloot (lit., with the heels over the ditch)	To make it by the skin of one's teeth.
hij loopt in geen zeven sloten tegelijk (lit., he doesn't walk in seven ditches simultaneously)	He can look after himself; no harm will come to him.
aan de dijk zetten (lit., to place on the dike)	to dismiss; to fire.
blijf met de klompen van 't ijs (lit., keep your wooden shoes off the ice)	keep out of it; mind your own business.
met de klompen op het ijs komen (lit., to go on the ice with wooden shoes)	to rush headlong into business; to butt in.

Nou breekt mijn klomp! (lit., now my wooden shoe breaks)	Good Lord! What next?
op je klompen aan- voelen (lit., to feel it with your wooden shoes)	it's obvious.
een klap van de molen hebben (lit., to get hit by the windmill)	to be crazy.
als 't schip met geld komt (lit., when the ship comes with money)	when my ship comes home.
recht door zee gaan (lit., to go straight through the sea)	to come straight to the point.
de bloemetjes buiten zetten (lit., to put the lit- tle flowers outside)	to paint the town red.
de bloemen staan op de ruiten (lit., the flowers are standing on the window panes)	the windows are frosted over.
iemand in de bloemetjes zetten (lit., to place someone in the little flowers)	to treat someone like a king/queen.

Chapter 17

FOOD FOR THOUGHT

(CULINARY CHARACTER)

Some Traditional Dishes

The international respect bestowed upon the Dutch cuisine is reflected in the abundance of Dutch restaurants found in London, Paris, Berlin, New York or Sydney.

Culinary orgasmic delights such as *stamppot* (mashed potato and cabbage) somehow do not entice the gentry as do *coq au vin à la bourguignonne* or *scaloppeine di vitello al Marsala*. And Edam *kaas* (cheese) is no match for *Caprice des Dieux* or *Swiss Gruyère*.

Appelgebak (Dutch apple pie) differentiates itself from other countries' traditional versions by the ritual around which it is consumed. Preferably accompanied by close friends, in a **gezellig café**, the **appelgebak** with or without **slagroom** (whipped cream), and cups of fresh, hot coffee, are slowly consumed, each mouthful garnished by deep and meaningful social intercourse.

Erwtensoep is Holland's ceremonial centrepiece, succulent starter, majestic main course . . . whatever. It consists of a delicious, thick pea soup infested with lumps of ham and vegetable(s). It is served with spoon and bib, and is available in kit-form at specialist shops, and in canned- and powdered-form at supermarkets. It's as close as you can get to a national dish, or national bowl.

Hutspot (meat, carrot and potato stew) is a hearty dish, about as exciting as such a stew can be. It is most popular in the winter months.

Uitsmijter (ham/cheese and 2 or 3 semi-fried eggs on untoasted toast) is mainly adopted as a lunchtime treat when even the Dutch cannot face the standard fare (see below).

Midday Morsels

The standard lunchtime **pièce de résistance** is a tantalising choice between open- or closed-sandwiches. *Cloggy* bread, which is rather dry and bland to the point of seeming stale, is lightly smeared with saltless butter or saltless margarine and topped with translucent slithers of processed ham or processed cheese. The saltless lubricant is probably an attempt to counteract the effect of the highly salted topping. (Edam cheese is salted during manufacture in order to give it a bit of taste.)

Their salt sandwiches are invariably eaten with a knife and fork, and are washed down with coffee or fruit juice to avoid dehydration.

The final course is typically 1 apple or 1 orange, peeled with the same knife that was used to dissect the main course. For an experience of poetry in motion, observe the way the Dutch peel their oranges.

Restaurants

Foreign restaurants are popular social gathering points in towns and cities. Italian, Greek, Chinese and Indonesian eating establishments are commonplace. Turkish, Indian and Mexican are breeding fast. Unfortunately, the dishes served are often corrupted by substitutes for certain non-obtainable original ingredients, as is the case in all European countries.

Dutch traditional restaurants also exist. They serve some or all of the dishes previously mentioned, and soup-up the attraction by including other European classics, such as *Wienerschnitzel, Jägerschnitzel*, steak (*biefstuk* — child's portion) and *Tartar* (raw minced meat, *rundergehakt*).

More important than the food is the *ambiance* that permeates the place. Basically, the cosier the climate, the more popular the establishment. If the *milieu* is to their liking, the Dutch do not mind forking out a little more than usual. The incredible atmosphere of many of the restaurants is reflected in the overall *décor*, due a *mélange* of all those wonderful and typical features touched upon in this work, such as flowers, plants, coffee, apple pie, cleanliness, music, friendliness of staff and price range. Lighting, furniture, architecture and style of plateware (porcelain, etc) are also important. Political, religious, or "good cause" affiliations are often used to lure customers; in these eating houses, posters and propaganda flavour the scene.

Whatever the locale, there is a definite etiquette that is followed when the meal arrives: Before commencing your meal, wish your companion(s) *bon appétit* by uttering one of the following: *eet smakelijk, smakelijk eten* or *eet ze*. And observe the "paying protocol".

The "paying protocol" prescribes that if you are invited out for a meal, you pay for yourself ("go dutch"). If someone else pays for your meal, reciprocate as soon as possible.

Snackbars

Snackbars introduced themselves in Holland long before the concept of "fast food" infested western culture.

Banks of coin-operated hatches (*automaten*) announce the presence of gastronomic goodies such as over- or under-cooked chicken *(kip)* wings, hamburgers, potato croquettes *(kroketten)* and fascinating noodle slabs. Together with the compulsory salted French Fries (swimming in mayonnaise), this type of convenient meal provides just the thing for a healthy jogger to feast on after a strenuous workout.

Perhaps more popular are the relatively new *Shoarma* snackbars, which identify themselves by the presence of a vertical grilling device (containing a rotary spit, heavily loaded with thin, wide slices of lamb) strategically located at the front of the ex-shop. These establishments assemble the middle-east version of hamburgers, consisting of dissected pita bread loaded with hackings from the spit, weeping green-salad components and a hot sauce, guaranteed to mask any natural flavour.

Tipp(le)ing

Many restaurants throughout Europe automatically include the tip in the bill. If no tip is included, standard Dutch practice is to leave a coin or two on the table, to express gratitude to the staff. Whereas a 10-cent tip is considered a grave insult outside Holland, it is considered a tremendous token of appreciation by Dutch restaurant clientele. We doubt this sentiment is also shared by the restaurant staff.

For those who prefer their sustenance in liquid form, and a little stronger than milk, Dutch bars are also places of intense social discourse and atmosphere. Some are open 24 hours a day, some daytime only, some evenings/nights.

If you drink alone, there is no chance of boredom as most bars provide a monumental display of curiosities and collections on their walls. If the bar has a history, you'll find it on the walls; if the owner has a history, you'll find it on the walls; if its name suggests a theme, you'll find it on the walls; and so on. If you find a bell hanging from a rope, or a rope hanging from a bell, don't ring it, despite possible encouragement from the locals. By doing so, you're agreeing to buy all present a drink of their choice!! Be cautious when using the phrase, "Let's have a drink" (*borrel* or *borreltje*), as it can easily be interpreted as, "The drinks are on me."

Dutch gin *(Genever)* can blow your head off! Dutch beer *(bier; pils)* is sweet, tasty and strong. Ordering a beer can be confusing for foreigners who attempt to do so for the first time in Dutch. No matter how you refer to a "beer" in Dutch, the bartender will respond by using a different term. Here, the obsession with diminutives (see Chapter 16) comes into play:

> *"Mag ik een bier?"* *("May I have a beer?")*
> *"Een biertje?"* *("A beer?")*
> *(lit., "A little beer?" – doesn't refer to size)*
>
> *"Mag ik een pils?"* *("May I have a beer?")*
> *"Een pilsje?"* *(" A beer?")*
> *(lit., "A little beer?" – doesn't refer to size)*

For a small glass of beer, use the double diminutive:

> *"Mag ik een kleintje pils?"* *(a "small beer")*
> *(lit., "May I have a small little beer?")*
> *"Een kleintje?"* *("A small one?")*
> *("A small little one?" – refers to size)*

Beer is generally served in small, flower-pot shaped glasses. When poured or pumped into these containers, a considerable amount of froth or "head" develops, which is sliced flush with the rim. The resultant offering often shocks European visitors. Germans laugh at the sawn-off "head" and protest the lack of quantity (as usual) while Brits laugh at the lack of quantity and protest the over-abundance of "head". French and Italians just drink it and think romantic thoughts of home.

Chapter 18

SEX 'N DRUGS
AND
ROCK 'N ROLL

Wealthy Dutchmen would rather talk about their sex lives than their money, and their sex lives are far less interesting.

> J. van Hezewijk,
> author *The Top Elite*
> *of the Netherlands*, 1987.

Let us remember that we have an open society, a nice, friendly clean country. We don't have the lethal terrorism other countries experience.

> Cees van Lede,
> President of the Federation
> of Netherlands Industry, 1987.

Every society, no matter how wealthy or puritanical, has its dark side. Having covered the finer elements of the Dutch in the 17 chapters preceding this, we now in conclusion turn to the more infamous aspects. The three major cities of Holland (Amsterdam, Rotterdam and The Hague) are cities for the young-at-heart, and the nucleus of open vice, crime and corruption. In the 80's, Amsterdam was proclaimed the CULTURAL capital of Europe; earlier, it acquired, and still retains, the status of GAY capital of Europe and DRUG capital of Europe.

In many rural areas, diluted forms of vice, crime and corruption are prevalent. In others, strict catholicism and other moral standards have stemmed the tide of indecency to the extent that cigarette vending machines are emptied at midnight on Saturdays to prevent trading on a Sunday.

Sex as an Activity

It has been said that the Dutch approach the subject of sex with the warmth and passion of an ice cube. Sex is an act society encourages of individuals aged 14 and up (in 1987, much pressure was applied to the government to lower the age of consent from 16 to 12 years). Many mothers monitor their young teenage daughters for signs of their first menstruation. This is the time to whisk the poor confused girl to her doctor for her first birth control kit. The male situation is quite different. At the first signs of pubescence, it is not unusual for a Dutch lad to be hounded by his father to experiment with sex, sometimes with no concern for the consequences.

These magnificent displays of understanding and tenderness sow the seeds of sex attitude in the developing children. By the time they reach adulthood, performing the sex act regularly is considered part of the daily routine; in the words of a housewife, "*Ja*, having sex is something you do in the morning and at night, like brushing your teeth."

Part of the Daily Routine

Sex can be mentioned coldly but candidly with dinner guests: "The children had fun at the beach yesterday. We had good sex last night. I must go to the dentist soon."

The subject of abortion (a *Vrouwen* birthright) is treated with similar nonchalance. "Did your period start yet?" "No, I had an abortion. On the way home, my Bicycle had a puncture . . ."

Sex as an Industry

Prostitution grew and flourished in the major cities from the lusting natures of seafarers arriving from long journeys. The Dutch, ever alert to the prospect of easy florins, soon established "red light districts" and even neighbourhoods for the plying of the prostitution trade. These areas have remained as such to this day. With the advent of sexual openness in the western world in the 60's, these areas have lost their sleaziness and become major tourist attractions. Prostitutes accept major credit cards, cheques, foreign currency — anything that represents MONEY.

They exude pride in their profession (making no attempt to disguise their business); attend regular, local-government-organized, medical check-ups; and enjoy a healthy relationship with the tax officials who will grant deductions for a range of occupational necessities.

The main opposition to open prostitution comes from the regiment of liberated **Vrouwen** (see Chapter 11) who view the emancipated, enterprising "ladies of pleasure" as a disease infecting the decent and honest Dutch way of life . . .

> **. . . . Thus, those who campaign for women's freedom and independence are the ones that object most severely to women having achieved that status.**

For those who prefer synthetic sex, the availability of all things pornographic is overwhelming. Sex shops are in such abundance that one can rarely pass through more than two streets in larger city interiors without spotting a shop window openly displaying devices, films, clothing and literature of a diverse sexual nature. Competition is so sharp that specialist sex shops (gay, lesbian, child, etc.) are also open for business.

Drugs

The drugs connection, and the Dutch over-tolerant attitude to drug abuse, are almost as famous as their tulips and windmills.

What seems shocking to tourists is run-of-the-(wind)mill for the Dutch. In Amsterdam, it is normal to see marijuana plants growing in homes and occasionally even in public places. The locals think nothing of smoking a "joint" in public. The Hash *Café (hasj-café)*, gloriously announced by a marijuana leaf painted on the front window and/or *café* sign, abounds. Ironically, many of these specialist *cafés* are not licensed to sell beverages of an intoxicating nature.

The current generation of *cloggies* are mavens in soft drugs. The Hash *Cafés* stock various varieties of seeds and young plants, soil enrichers and pots; the proprietor being only too willing to guide a customer in his purchase, by process of elimination based on the anticipated growing-environment:

- Indoors, outdoors, greenhouse
- Harvesting time
- Direction of prevailing natural light
- Soil.

Hard drugs are less openly traded. The merchants comprise an army of solicitors of various minority groups who hustle for customers at main railway stations, monuments, public parks, youth centres, red light districts, etc. In theory, possession of hard drugs is illegal. In practice,

users are not arrested; only the (bulk) dealers are liable for prosecution.

For some years, an "innovative approach" was to give the dealers and junkies their own part of town – the Zeedijk in Amsterdam – where they were allowed to do business. The idea was to be kind and open to dealers and junkies while concentrating their activities to a specific area. The result? In the words of Eduard van Thijn, then Mayor of Amsterdam, *"We thought we could be tolerant and still control hard drugs. We were very naive."*

Crime and Punishment

Convictions for drug trafficking (and other criminal activities) are sometimes never served. With prisons stocked to capacity and due to the Dutch tendency towards forgiveness, sentences are often extremely lenient. Prison terms are served on a space availability basis. Thus, a criminal (sorry, "victim of society") will be released upon conviction, pending an empty cell. If a criminal does go to jail, chances are his or her stay will be carried out in relative comfort. The idea is to provide the prisoners with as normal a lifestyle as possible. At Schutterswei, a jail in Alkmaar, prisoners are paid around HFl 55- a week. Many use the money to decorate and furnish their private "cells" with televisions, stereos, pets and, of course, a *koffie*-maker. A special private visitor's room – "sex cell" – is provided, complete with furniture (including a bed), paintings and carpet. Other privileges, or in this case rights, include wearing one's own clothing, access to a kitchen to cook one's own meals if so desired, the right to vote, freedom to speak to journalists and a system for expressing and debating complaints.

It is part design and part necessity that the Dutch have instigated forms of "alternative punishment" and "educational projects" in order to rehabilitate their "victims of society". Such forms of punishment may include a 22-day excursion to a mountain camp on the Mediterranean coast, enjoying the local countryside and cuisine.

Consequently, theft from automobiles is commonplace, as is pickpocketing and similar crimes. To have your car broken into and the HFl 500 radio-cassette player stolen is considered no big event.

The attitude of the police? One of inconvenience — your ex-property will be on sale in a bar the next evening where you can buy it back for HFl 60, and you must be grateful for such a bargain!

Rock 'n Roll, etc. . . .

It must be said that the Dutch are, as a nation, appreciative of music — contemporary and otherwise. Cities and towns provide a wealth of music venues to suit all tastes and (sub)cultures. Even small villages sport at least one location where varied, live music can be heard.

Music lovers? Yes. Innovators? No. *Cloggies* love to copy. Be it classical, traditional, modern or free-form jazz, they will copy recognized, accomplished performers to the last semi-quaver. In Amsterdam alone, one can walk along the inner-city shopping precincts on a Saturday and revel in a multiplicity of street- and *café*-musicians including at least:

- one Dutch highland bagpiper, complete with full Scots regalia of bearskin, tunic and kilt/sporran
- one Dutch traditional Irish session group, equipped with fiddles, mandolins, bones, bodhran drums and pints of Guinness
- one Dutch Mozart string quartet, optionally dressed in jeans or tails, and displaying music stands containing faded, manuscript, sheet music
- dozens of contemporary-bard stereotypes of the 1960's Dylan/Donovan variety, equipped with aging acoustic guitar and tattered guitar case (covered in stickers) at their feet for "contributions".

Yet Holland is a country for the young at heart. And the food of youth is Rock 'n Roll.

In Amsterdam, Rock venues abound, openly selling mainly-imported Hard Rock music, alcohol and drugs to the age group 16+. Inaptly described as "multi-media centres" or "youth clubs", the more infamous include the Paradiso and the Melkweg in the equally infamous Leidseplein area. Rotterdam and The Hague have their equivalents. On a less lavish scale, but by no means small in number are the Rock *Cafés* – bars steaming with "heavy metal" fans who drink, smoke and dope their way to oblivion, nightly, between the hours of 8pm and 2am. The drink is the locally-brewed Heineken or Amstel pilsner beer, the smoke-and-dope is mainly cigarettes (Camel brand for the males and liberated females, Pall Mall for the females and liberated males), marijuana and hashish. All washed down with lashings of hot Rock music, provided via the medium of modern, high-quality, Japanese electronics.

A wandering minstrel

Appendix A

A View of the Dutch Through the English Language

Dutch **auction**	an auction that proceeds backwards; one in which the price is reduced until a buyer is found.[2]
Dutch **bargain**	bargain made and sealed while drinking.[3]
beat the *Dutch*	to do something extraordinary or startling. Ex: How does he do it? It beats the Dutch.[1]
Dutch **built**	originally Dutch flat-bottomed vessels[1]; current usage attibuted to (a) male: long and lanky (b) female: see Dutch buttocked.
Dutch **buttocked**	originally, a strain of Dutch cattle with large hind quarters[1]; contemporary association is the large, pear-shaped rump of modern Dutch women, stemming from excessive bicycle riding and dairy products.
Dutch **consolation**	the philosophy or attitude that, "Whatever ill befalls you, there is someone worse off than you[1]".
Dutch **courage**	courage induced by alcoholic drink.[2]
do a *Dutch*	to desert, escape; to commit suicide.[1]
double *Dutch*	gibberish.[1]
Dutch **feast**	a party where the entertainer gets drunk before his guests.[1]

*dutch*ing	the use of gamma rays to make spoiled food edible again.[4]
*dutch*man	an object for hiding faulty workmanship (construction).
go *Dutch*	to have each person pay his own expenses.
(I'm a) *Dutch*man	a phrase implying refusal or disbelief.[2]
in *Dutch*	in disfavour, disgrace or trouble.[1]
Dutch **lottery**	a lottery in which tickets are drawn in certain classes or series for each of which certain prizes increasing in number and value with each class are fixed.[3]
Dutch **metal**	a malleable alloy . . . beaten into thin leaves, and used as cheap imitation of gold-leaf; also called "Dutch gold", "Dutch foil" and "Dutch leaf." [1]
Dutch **oven**	a person's mouth.[1]
to *Dutch*	to miscalculate in placing bets so as to have a mathematical expectancy of losing rather than winning.[3]
Dutch **treat**	a party, outing, etc. at which each participant pays for his own share (corruption of "Dutch trait").[2]
Dutch **uncle**	a severe critic or counsellor.

1 The Oxford Dictionary, Clarendon Press, 1989, Vol. IV, p. 1140-1141.
2 The Oxford Reference Dictionary, Clarendon Press, 1986, p. 253.
3 By permission. From Webster's Third New International Dictionary © 1986 by Merriam-Webster Inc., publisher of the Merriam-Webster® dictionaries.
4 Volkskrant, July 1990.

Appendix B

A Chosen Selection of Dutch/English Homonyms

Incorrect use of the Dutch/English homonyms can have an interesting effect on people. At an informal get-together, one Dutch woman introduced herself to a British woman. When asked about her profession, the Dutch woman calmly stated, "I fuck dogs."

Here is a selection of some of the more disastous cases:

Dutch word	Sounds like	English word
bil	(buttocks)	bill
dier	(animal)	dear
fiets	(bicycle)	feats/feets
fok	(breed)	fuck
heet	(to be named)	hate
hoor	(hear)	whore
keek	(looked)	cake
kont	(buttocks)	cunt
kwik	(quick)	mercury
mais	(corn)	mice
peen	(carrot)	pain
reep	(rope, line)	rape
rente	(account-interest)	rent
rits	(zipper)	Ritz
rood	(red)	road
slim	(clever)	slim

Dutch word	Sounds like	English word
slip	(underpants)	slip
snoep	(sweets, candy)	snoop
strip	(comic book)	strip
toneel	(theater-play)	toenail
vaart	(travel, sail)	fart
vlaai	(fruit pie/tart)	fly

Appendix C

In Case You
Don't Believe Us . . .

A load of . . .(mountains of manure in the Netherlands),
The Economist, March 14, 1987, p. 46.

Doing Time the Dutch Way
World Press Review, May 1988, p. 53.

Draagbaar Homomonument (Portable Homo-Monument)
de Volkskrant, 24 November 1988.

Dutch Treat
Forbes, July 2, 1985, p. 31.

Europe's Least Awful Prisons (Dutch Jails)
The Economist, February 6, 1988, p. 17-19.

Flower Power: Everything's coming up tulips in the
Netherlands
Newsweek, May 5, 1986, p. 42-43.

Holland: Drawing The Line, Has Permissiveness Gone
Too Far?
Time, August 10, 1987
(European edition), front cover & p. 18-24.

Holland Suffers From an Acute Case of Eurosclerosis
Business Month, March 1989, p. 30-31.

Institutional Tolerance of Marijuana in Holland
Whole Earth Review, Spring 1987, p. 58-59.

Money Seems to Grow on Tulips
Fortune, October 12, 1987, p. 180-181.

Plenty of let and hindrance
The Economist, September 17, 1988, p. 53.

Shrewd Managers of Regal Riches
Fortune, October 12, 1987, p. 134-35.

The Pope on Hostile Soil
Newsweek, May 13, 1985, p. 35.

The Pope's Dutch Welcome
Newsweek, May 27, 1985, p. 8-10.

The War on Plant Theft
Maclean's, June 10, 1985, p. 65-66.

The Dutch Touch
National Geographic, October 1986, p. 501-525.

Tolerance Finally Finds Its Limits
Time, August 31, 1987 (USA edition), p. 28-29.

Too Good to Last (Dutch welfare benefits)
The Economist, March 30, 1985, p. 62-63.